"An Inquiring Mind, Life's Challenges, and God's Surprises"

I Remember...

THOUGHTS ON A WELL-LIVED LIFE

By Robert William Lawrenz

Xulon
PRESS

I Remember...
by Robert William Lawrenz
rlawrenz@comcast.net

Associate Editor: Roger Luoma
Cover Design by: Elizabeth Luoma

Printed in the United States of America

ISBN 9781609571481

www.xulonpress.com

I Remember is a delightful combination of practical wisdom and interesting adventures told in a very entertaining way. As Bob Lawrenz tells about his personal experiences and his commitment to Jesus Christ one cannot miss the strong character traits of honesty, integrity and faithfulness that make his story compelling. I treasure my long friendship with Bob and found myself thinking, "Yes, that's Bob," as I read in chapter after chapter his impressive record of accomplishments in various fields of endeavor, always with the motivation of serving God by serving people.

—Don Treash

∾

Bob's legacy writing—*I Remember*—remarkably explains the blessed life of one who commits himself to the Lord and follows His guidance in all paths of his life. Bob illustrates his commitment in the orderly fashion of his life—to first choose to love the Lord with all his heart; then to honor, love and respect Lura as God's gift to him in marriage; to earnestly teach Dawn, Bill and Carla the ways of the Lord, to link his life together in Church leadership; and to live his business life with Christian rules and integrity. Through these five decades of our friendship together, I have valued Bob's friendship, respected the ways he has served others in Jesus' Name and love and delight to be called 'Bob's friend'.

—Frank Doten

Dedication

This book is dedicated to my dear wife Lura.
Her encouragement has made my life a
dream come true. I love thee my Lura.

I Remember...

Contents

Family Life

Adventure

Afterthoughts

Prologue

For a number of years now my son Bill has urged me to write my life story because my life has been so eventful. I must admit I have a "profound sense of priority and did not want to undertake such a formidable task, choosing instead to write "Life In Focus" with 50 insights into life, a Time Line of all the significant events of our lives and a Family Tree, with over fifteen hundred entries. But I feel now is the time to write my life story.

I am old enough now to see life in retrospect, which is a quality of maturing, that only comes with time. Many people have told me that I have the gift of wisdom Wisdom is the application of knowledge and the understanding of how things work. So, I decided to tell my story and let you be the judge of whether I have applied wisdom to my life.

My approach is to tell my story in three parts – first, my life aside from our foreign travel and my military experience and business career, then special sections to cover those experiences and finally my observations on life. In certain sensitive areas I have changed the names to protect confidentiality of those who have entrusted me with their private lives.

The content and ideas of a book comes from the author but the quality of a book is the editing. Roger Luoma, Marlene Warden, Crystal Engel, Dawn Sjolund and Lura devoted their time and expertise to editing this book. Roger Luoma assisted with his expertise in the preparation of this book. I am greatly indebted to them

My memoirs, Time Line, Family Tree and Life in Focus Insights are my legacy to future generations. These are my way of passing on my knowledge, understanding and wisdom to my children and grandchildren. As I mature, Family takes on a whole new meaning.

Robert William Lawrenz

Family Life
CHAPTER I

The Early Years.... as I Remember Them

Train up a child in the way he should go,
Even when he is old he will not depart from it.
— Proverbs 22:6

Join me in a Tom Sawyer-Huckleberry Finn boyhood; a business career that lasted fifty years including playing crime detective; dealing with an extortionist; confronting government bureaucrats; mentoring 100 business clients; living under the threat of the North Korean army on the Korean DMZ; settling dozens of Laotian refugees in the U.S. and traveling to exotic places in 30 countries, including Black Water Rafting in New Zealand. This was accomplished while being a faithful husband to a devoted wife, father of three children, and grandfather of four granddaughters. Join me on a life well lived as I remember it.

My life was traditional. Born the only child of parents who loved each other until death, I attended public schools, took Jesus into my heart, lived in a middle class neighborhood in a middle class family with middle class values, went off to college, spent two years in the military, started a business career that would last forty years, married a godly woman and that marriage would last over fifty years, had three children, then four grandchildren and retired. Yes, very, very traditional. It has been the most fun, meaningful, rewarding and adventurous life one could hope for. God was in it all and I anticipate hearing,

"Enter into my kingdom, my good and faithful servant."

I was born in Chicago, Illinois, in St. Anne's hospital on July 12, 1932, the only child of Ambrose Lawrenz and Margaret Cavanaugh and the first child ever born there with platinum blond hair. As an only child I was pampered and could do no wrong. I felt undeserving, but over time this would change as I gained independence and self-confidence.

My earliest memory, when I was just five years old, is my grandfather's funeral. I remember entering a shed-type of building with rough flooring and seeing him in a wooden box that was too small for him.

Years later my father confirmed my recollection and explained that the family was too poor to afford a traditional funeral. The coffin was unsalable because it was too small for most people, but Grandpa

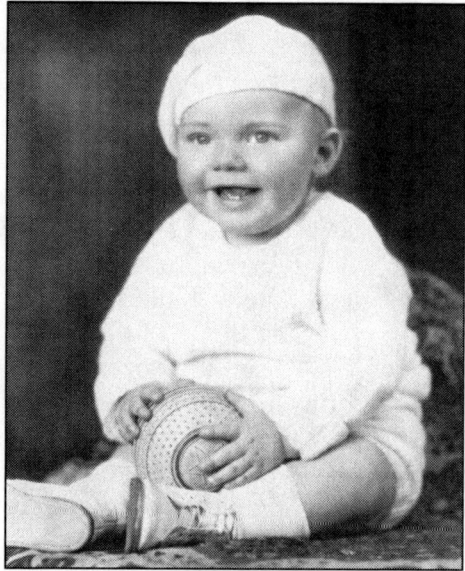

9 months old and pampered.

was a small man so they bought it at an affordable price.

His three sons, Ambrose, Herbert, and Charles, had to dig the grave because it was during the economic depression of the 1930's and there was no extra money even for a burial. They were not the exception; almost everyone was poor and for those who lived through it, it would have a lasting impact on their actions and outlook on life. Unlike my father, my two uncles lived thereafter fearing a return to hard times all of their lives and were afraid to invest.

As a young child my career dream was to be a garbage collector. I would sit on the garbage bins at the back of the property and wait for the collectors to come through our alley. I was fascinated by the garbage wagons pulled by horses.

I have a faint recollection of my uncle Les coming to our apartment. He was an alcoholic and would come occasionally for a warm bath, a clean set of underwear and a good meal. My mother was a caring person and very devoted to the family.

Between 3 and 4 years old.

My next remembrance is of going to kindergarten for the first time. My mother drove me to school, watched me enter school and drove home. I went in the school door but quickly exited the building and returned home to my mother's surprise. I had decided not to go to kindergarten but go directly to college like Tom Berk, my neighbor and idol.

After kindergarten we moved from Lockwood Avenue to 1408 Lorel Avenue. This was only one block away but it required me to change to the Ella Flag Young Grade School. I do not remember anything about the school except one day while playing at recess we panicked a horse that was pulling a milk wagon and he took off. In those days the milkman would take enough bottles of milk to serve several houses and the horse was trained to continue going down the street to meet the milkman at the end of his route. Life on Lorel Avenue lasted about 3 years but during those years I had lots of fun, running with a gang of neighborhood kids. We called ourselves "The Lorel Gang". One of my favorite activities was to go several blocks away from home to play in the railroad switching yard, which was very dangerous so I did not tell my parents about it. I remember being chased by the railroad police but they never caught us. Another favorite activity was playing "waterfall." This consisted of going down the alley and finding tin cans of various sizes. We would punch one hole in the bottom near the

I was 9 years old in 1941. The apartment building is where our family lived on the second floor. Our close friends the Wades lived on the first floor.

edge. Then we place the cans on the stairs so the hole would extend over the edge and over the can on the lower step. Now we were ready for the fun. We would pour water into the top can and watch it pass down from can to can. If the system was not balanced there would be a crisis and water would escape.

Inside I played war with toy soldiers in forts built of blocks on the dining room table. Every afternoon I would listen to my favorite radio programs, Tom Mix, Jack Armstrong and the Lone Ranger for over an hour. After the last radio program I would patiently stand by the window waiting for my father to come home from work.

My best friend Jimmy Wade and I worked out a system whereby we could get our parents' consent for us to go anywhere or do anything. We would go to one mother and ask permission and the usual answer was, "No"; then we would ask if the other mother approved could we go and the answer was usually, "Yes".

We would then go to the other mother and ask for permission and say it was okay with the first mother for us to go, so her answer was usually "yes." If the mothers compared notes, we never knew it. We traveled all over the city of Chicago as young boys without fear.

I remember one afternoon my mother telling me that the Japanese had bombed Pearl Harbor and we were at war - it was December 7, 1941. America's industry retooled to produce war materials at an astonishing rate; everyone pitched in, even growing vegetables in Victory Gardens. My mother went to work at the Douglas aircraft factory and I did my part by collecting newspapers and scrap metal and by buying $.25 stamps to purchase War Bonds. The country was totally united and remained so until there was a total victory. While it was a war that covered the entire world it lasted only four years because we were committed to win. That generation of people would be known as "The Greatest Generation", having survived both the world war and the great depression.

THE WADE FAMILY

The Wade family and our family were the closest of friends, even closer than kin, for many years. We lived in the same apartment building – upstairs and downstairs – and our mothers even used our kids telegraph system to communicate rather than having to use the stairs every time they wanted to talk. Marion and Lil Wade had two children, Jim and Mary, who were like a brother and sister to me, so I never felt like an only child. Every Sunday night the two mothers would put the three kids to bed and the two men would take Marion's mother, a devoted Christian woman, to Moody Church on the north side of Chicago.

After a while the men got tired of waiting for Marion's mother and decided to sit in the back of the church. There they heard Dr. Harry Ironsides preach. When they returned home to play bridge they talked about what they heard at church. The two women were both devout practicing Catholics and found the discussion of spiritual things interesting because they had never heard about accepting Christ as personal savior. To them being a good Christian was going to mass and confession. After a few visits to church the two men went down the aisle to accept Christ as their Lord and Savior and then shared their experience with their wives. Soon the two women personalized their faith and they all began a life of sharing Christ and stewardship.

All three of us kids lived in homes where God was an integral part of life and were taken to church regularly, so accepting Christ as my own personal savior was natural. The zeal of new life in Christ was evident in our parents' lives and things would never be the same.

Marion Wade was a fascinating personality, being a frustrated minor league baseball catcher with a very competitive spirit. His competitive spirit and entrepreneurial bent would lead him from being a poor, struggling one-man carpet cleaning service to a multi-millionaire as owner of Service Master Corporation. After World II the trend in home furnishings went from using rugs to wall to wall carpeting. When the carpeting became soiled it had to be pulled up, sent out to a rug cleaning plant and then re-installed. This was an aggravating and costly problem and the carpet would never fit like it originally did. Marion developed a method of cleaning the carpet in place by using a shampoo that separated the soil from the carpet fiber.

Even though he had an average intelligence he had good insights into people and hired a great team of employees. Marion was the P.R. man and leader; Ken Hansen, a preacher turned businessman operated the business; Art Melvin was the super salesman to whom you could not say, "No"; and Ray Hass was the chemist. Marion also hired a number of young men returning from the war who were highly motivated because they had young families. In spite of his rise to wealth he remained a committed Christian and gave the Lord credit for his success, giving millions to the Lord's work. As he became wealthier and wealthier the Wades' lifestyle changed and the relationship with my parents finally ended. I never knew what the Wades did to hurt my parents' feelings, but my parents ended the relationship of 25 years.

Marion Wade's life story is recorded in his book "The Lord Is My Counsel." (Prentice-Hall, 1987).
On September 8, 2001 the Marion Wade Center was dedicated on the campus of Wheaton College, Wheaton, Illinois. It features the personal memorabilia of the Christian authors C.S. Lewis, J.R.R. Tolkien and G. K. Chesterton, including Lewis's writing desk and the famous chest that was the inspirition for the "Witch and the Wardrobe".

THE WAR YEARS

In 1942 we moved to the very northwest section of Chicago, Edison Park, and lived at 7408 Palatine Avenue in a new house, the first home my parents had owned. The war was underway; construction of houses was being curtailed so my parents were fortunate to be able to buy a newly constructed home. The only restrictions were that common brick be used for the outside walls and the number of electrical outlets was limited. I remember seeing it under construction. The house cost $6,000 and had a 10% down payment. My mother, with the $600 down payment cash in her purse, left for the closing. Not realizing she had left her purse on top of the car, she drove off. Fortunately she discovered it and returned to find it but, it was a near death experience because my father would not have been very understanding of such carelessness. At that time in his life he had a short fuse.

I entered the fourth grade at Norwood Park Grade School and struggled as a student who did not like school. In the sixth grade Mrs. Colin realized that I could not read or spell. She sent me to the office where Miss Notes taught me phonics. It was like the lights went on as I learned "a" was "ah", and "b" was "ba" because I had been taught with the "look/say" method where you look at a word and remember what it means, how to pronounce it and how to spell it. My problem was that I could not retain the words. I would get nearly 100 percent on the weekly spelling tests but 30 percent on the year-end final. From then on, with my new skills, my life began to improve. I have never understood why educators, with the benefit of a phonic language, would teach English any other way than phonetically. While schools no longer use the look/say method, I believe the reason home-schooled students test so well is the fact that most are taught phonics.

One reason I enjoyed my childhood was the neighborhood friends. There were endless games of kick-the-can and capture-the-flag. Another of my favorite things was taking my dog Ginger for a run in the three whole blocks of prairie near our home. He was an English Setter who would run for hours and occasionally flush out a pheasant or rabbit. The three blocks of prairie were partially developed years before in the late 1920's with sewer lines. We kids discovered the unused sewer pipes and would crawl through them for long distances. It was a good thing my parents did not know about our secret tunnels.

Another thing I really enjoyed was being able to help care for three horses kept in a barn adjacent to our property. Mr. Overhill was

In 1946, on my 8th Grade graduation day.

a City of Chicago politician who owned property that was not on any street so it could not be developed for residential homes. It was, however, suitable for a barn and paddock. One of the horses was a Trotter (alternating front leg forward; back leg backward) named Mr. Scott, the second a mare, Pacer (alternating front leg forward; back leg forward) and the third was Pacer's colt named Cynthia. The horses would race pulling a sulky. I developed a love for horses as I fed, curried and rode them.

As in many a neighborhood, there was a crabby family

who we kids did not like. We decided to pull a prank on them by placing a firecracker in their mailbox. The mailbox was the type built into the wall of the house that had an outer flap, a passageway though the wall and a small wooden door on the inside. One night we dropped a lit firecracker into the mailbox and ran a short distance but did not hear the firecracker go off. Then there was a loud explosion and we ran for blocks before stopping for a rest. We found out later that the explosion blew the inner door of the box right off its hinges and across the room. I am sure they knew who did it, but there were no repercussions.

During my grade school days we attended the Bethel Bible Church where our family and the Wades were very active. The church pastor was Ken Hansen, succeeded by Lyle York. Those two and Billy Graham, who all became close friends while students at Wheaton College, were invited to our home for dinner. I remember my mother fixing one of her delicious meals and the three young men eating multiple helpings. Each of these men would go on to change the world for Christ. Ken became CEO of Service Master which would contribute hundreds of millions of dollars to God's work; Lyle would be a missionary to Japan during the historic restoration period following World War II; and Billy who would lead more people to Christ than any other person in the history of Christianity. Meanwhile the church was growing and needed more space. A house in Chicago was given to the church and moved section by section to a site across the street from the church. Each section was numbered to help facilitate the building's re-assembly by volunteers. There was a naming contest for the new building and I won with the name "Beth-Haven."

∽

HIGH SCHOOL

I graduated in 1946 from Norwood Park Grade School and entered William Howard Taft High School. While I hated grade school, high school was tolerable. I only worked hard enough to get passing grades but I took the most difficult courses, four years of math and four years of science. One of my teachers was Dr. Donetski, who was an "air-head." We loved to play tricks on him.

Once while he was out of the classroom one of the boys looked at the test answers on his desk and wrote them on the blackboard. On the test everyone got 100 percent right, which rattled him, so we told him what we had done. He wanted to know who wrote the answers on the board and offered extra points to anyone who would tell him who the guilty party was. We negotiated the reward points up to a higher level, a reprieve for the culprit, and then the culprit turned himself in to get the points.

One spring day when all the windows in our second floor classroom were open, one of the boys who was sitting in the back row near the door sneaked outside and sprawled down on the ground under the windows of the classroom. At a prearranged time one of the boys in the class began shouting, "he fell, he fell," as he leaned out of the window. The teacher ran to the window and looked out to see the student on the ground. Then the boy stood up to the surprise of the teacher. Why Dr. Donetski did not have a heart attack I will never know. Another event of note was my chemistry class where there were pipes supplying gas and water to the lab tables. Some of the boys connected the water line to the gas line. Since water pressure was greater than gas pressure, the gas lines got full of water, and when the water reached the boiler room there was big trouble. Several of the boys were expelled and did not graduate, but I had nothing to do with that prank.

In my high school years I changed churches and attended the Norwood Park Baptist Church. There was a Christian Service Brigade club that was a major influence in my life. The Miller brothers, Mel and Mannard, were my role models and helped shape my leadership skills. In addition to our weekly meetings we had baseball and basketball teams. One year I was voted most valuable player, but our teams were not outstanding.

During my high school years I was very active in the church. I was president of the church young people's group with 30 to 40 in attendance. In addition to our regular Sunday night meetings we had an endless number of activities such as ice skating and tobogganing in the winter, picnics and trips to the Indiana sand dunes in the summer and formal dinners at the country club where all the girls wore formal gowns. During these years I had three close friends, Lu Tulga, George French and Gordy Hines. We had great times together including a camping/canoe trip down the Kalamazoo River to the City of Saugatuck on Lake Michigan. These years were a great time of learning and confirming my leadership skills. There are two types of leaders, natural or cultivated. I was a cultivated leader and a slow learner, but over the years I would develop and become comfortable with my own style of leadership.

෴

COLLEGE

Although I hated grade school and tolerated high school, I loved the college challenge. At the University of Illinois they graded on the curve. That meant that 10 percent would get "E's" and 20 percent would get "D's". This was not a problem in the first two years when there were 200 in a class but by the third and fourth year there were only 30 survivors in a class and 9 would get failing grades, creating a ruthless environment. Aside from all the things I learned, the one lesson I learned in college was to be a rational thinker. This would shape my thinking skills. While I studied all the time, I got "C's" and sometimes a "B".

One day after a class on Marketing I began comparing notes with my classmate Don Treash. We went to the coffee shop together and soon discovered we were both Christians. We developed a friendship that continues to this day, more than 50 years later. One of the few extra-curricular things I participated in was InterVarsity Christian Fellowship. There I found good role models like Freddy Gildes who was working on his doctor's degree to improve the status and image of Christians who were looked down upon by the academic world. Now Christians are academically superior but still looked down upon because of Post-Modernism and politically correct thinking that saturates the academic community. It never ceases to amaze me how intelligent men can be so blind to the plain truth.

One summer I went to Bear Trap Ranch with a group of classmates. It was a fun time and also a confirmation of my leadership skills through advanced training. At my college graduation ceremony John Kennedy, then a Senator, but soon to become President, was the speaker. These were defining years.and I would go on to marriage and a career. God had a wonderful plan for my life.

Family Life

CHAPTER II

Mid-life Years in Chicago
.... as I Remember Them

Trust in the Lord with all your heart
and do not lean on your own understanding.
In all your ways, acknowledge Him,
And He will make your paths straight.
— Proverbs 3:5 & 6

I was 25 years old and in early 1957 there were three defining events in my life.

First was my graduation from the University of Illinois from the College of Business with a major in Finance and a minor in Economics, a dream come true for my parents who had primed me for college since I was a child. They wanted me to be the first in the family to have a college education because my father only had a grade school education and knew first hand how difficult it was to advance in business without a degree.

Second was the start of my business career with a job at the Bell

My parents had primed me, and I had a finance degree.

& Howell Company *(Chapter VII)*. Third was meeting Lura, my wife-to-be, for the second time. With college and the military service *(Chapter VI)* behind me I felt free to get serious about a future mate. God would have great plans for me.

$\sim$

LURA ENTERS MY LIFE

My friend Gordy Hines invited me to go with him to an InterVarsity Bible study at the Moody Church in Chicago, the same church where my father found Christ. He was there to lead a study for a group of college students and student nurses from Swedish Covenant Hospital.

After the study Gordy and I asked two girls, who needed transportation back to the nurse's dorm, to go out for pizza. Lura Alexander was one of the girls and she said she had seen me before. After comparing histories we found that we had met three years before in a church in Manhattan, Kansas, while I was in the Army. She remembered me, but because she was a high school student at that time I had not taken special note of her. In conversation we found that we had a number of common friends.

God had brought us back together again even though I had missed on the first round. I called and asked Lura for a date and we went to a bicycling race at the Amphitheater in Chicago. The plan was to double date with Gordy, but we never found him. We spent two hours watching the bikes go around and around the track while we talked. It was not love at first sight, but after the first date it was a relationship I definitely wanted to pursue. We dated regularly and it was not long before I knew that I loved Lura and wanted her to be my companion for life. At first she had concerns because she was in nursing school with one and a half years left and there were restrictions on dating and marriage.

On one occasion I had called Lura and arranged to pick her up at the nurses' dorm. When I arrived I was greeted by a stern older woman who said that she would not call Lura because she had worked the night before and needed her undisturbed sleep. I tried to explain that I had talked with Lura on the phone and she was expecting me. As I reached across the desk to use the call board, she slapped my hand. Not to be deterred, I went to the local store and called Lura to come down and meet me at the door.

The first test of our relationship came when she returned home to Ohio during summer break. We wrote letters every day. One day the postman delivered mail to her house but there was no letter from me. As she watched the mailman go down the street she noticed him turn around and come back to deliver a special package from me. I had written a letter on a roll of adding machine paper with the first sentence extending down the full length of the scroll, which required her to role the scroll up to read the second sentence and so on. Lura still has that letter.

The second test of our relationship came when she was assigned to the Cook County Hospital on the south side of Chicago for four months as part of her training and I lived in the far northwest part of the city. By this time we were deeply in love and wanted to be together every day and Lura needed my emotional support. Since there were no expressways completed at that time, it required a one and a half hour drive each way. On the drive home I would have to stop and rest my eyes because I was so tired. I would also drive with the car windows open so I would not fall asleep. After several months I got infectious mono because my system was so run down.

While Lura was assigned to the hospital, my uncle, George Wulfram, who was married to May Cavanaugh, was admitted as a patient there because of dementia, but Lura discovered from looking at his chart he was being treated for alcoholism. Lura was a heroine with the family for getting the correct diagnosis. This opened the door for my mother to re-establish her relationship with her family

Our wedding in September 1958 . . . .

It was the start of a life of adventure, challenges and great blessings. We went from there to honeymoon at the Mohonk Resort in New York's Catskill Mountains, where we got up to our room on a rope elevator.

The wedding party – From left: Bridesmaids Norma Rogers/McHelheny, Lyn Alexander/Ambacher and Kathy Smail/Pederson, the bride and groom, and groomsmen Don Treash, Bill Becker and John Alexander.

which had been strained ever since she had given up being Catholic, a betrayal of a core value of the Cavanaugh family. My parents thought Lura was wonderful and just the right person for me to marry. Lura's parents also approved so we had both parents' blessing.

After a few months of dating we were looking forward to engagement and marriage. I returned from a vacation in Colorado and brought her a gift which was in a small ring-sized box. I wanted her to guess what was in it but she was suspicious and would not guess. I gave her a hint, it was metal and stone, but she still declined to guess. It was a piece of gold ore I had picked up while visiting a gold mine in Colorado. A short time later I would give her a ring-sized box with a diamond ring in it. I proposed and she graciously accepted. There was no doubt that Lura was meant for me and I for her, with both of our parents supporting our decision. Because Lura was restricted from getting married before graduation by her nursing school, we set September 13, 1958, as our wedding date. She finished school in August and took her State of Illinois exam to become a Registered Nurse in October.

But our wedding almost did not happen. Before the wedding I forgot to tell the best man to pick Lura up at our apartment. As time was running out she began to panic, but then realized that we could not have a wedding without a bride. It seems humorous now, but at the time it was not.

Our wedding party consisted of the bridesmaids - Lura's sister Lyn Alexander/Ambacher and two friends from nursing school, Norma Rogers/ McHelheny and Kathy Smail/Pederson - and Groomsmen - Lura's brother John Alexander and two college friends of mine, Don Treash and Bill Becker. Lura's brother Paul Alexander officiated.

Every wedding has its snafus and our wedding had two. We wanted to tape record our wedding ceremony so I assigned Dan the task of setting up the recorder in the sanctuary close to where we would take our vows. Lura, knowing Dan's track record, felt sure he would goof it up

in some way no matter how simple I made it. I assured her
all he had to do was plug it in and turn it on. Shortly after
the ceremony began we smelled smoke and I knew where
it was coming from. It was not Holy Smoke, it was the
jammed tape recorder. I learned from the very start to trust
Lura's wise judgment. The second problem was that Lura
and I memorized our vows rather than having the preacher
leads us through them. Half way through, the stress got to
us and we both forgot them. We both made up the last
lines and no one knew the difference.

After the wedding and reception our secret getaway plan
worked perfectly. It was the custom for the wedding party
to follow the car of the bride and groom. We had prearranged for our driver to go down a dead-end street where
our getaway car was parked just beyond a wall barricading
traffic. We were off to the A-B-C Motel without honking
cars following us.

On our honeymoon we visited Aunt Sarah Shattuck in
Philadelphia, and stayed at the George Washington Motel
where Lura used her maiden name when calling room
service. I had fun teasing her that she was now married and
should use my name. We also visited Valley Forge where
George Washington camped during the winter of 1777-
1778. The rest of our time was spent at beautiful Mohonk
Resort, located in the Catskill Mountains of up-state New
York. It seemed like we were the only guests under 80
years old.

We went up to our room using a rope elevator, and
found our room had two single beds. Every morning we
messed up the unused bed to make the maid think it had
been used. I remember one night going to a program on
bird calls, "WHOO WHOO", "KAU KAU" and "TWEET
TWEET." It did turn out to be interesting and fun. We
hiked around the beautiful lake and grounds.

We returned home to our apartment on 5801 Magnolia
Street in Chicago and set up housekeeping with the purchase of furniture from the Hufford Furniture Company
where we were able to purchase good quality furniture at

a discount. Fifty years later we still have some of the furniture and it is still in good condition. We faithfully attended the Edgewater Baptist Church where we had been married until we moved to Rolling Meadows a year later.

~

Lura began working as a nurse for a doctor with offices on Michigan Avenue. He was an endocrinologist with prestigious clients like Glenn Ford, the movie star. He would code their charts for security reasons. He was a good doctor and a good teacher with a staff that worked well together. Lura, who is good at building long-term relationships, recently met with Laurie, the medical secretary, after forty years of being apart. Evidence of Lura's building loving long-term relationships is last year she received 17 birthday cards. I received one from my insurance agent. While I may be understating the number of cards I received, the point is it better to be loved than respected. Over the years we benefited from

Graduate nurse Lura wearing her cap.

our decision for Lura to complete nurses training because she was able to supplement our income a number of times. She worked part time for Doctor Cluxton after first child, Dawn, was born, for the Winnebago County Health

Department in pediatric care for seven years and as a Health & Safety Nurse at Woodward Governor Company for seven years. She occasionally has breakfast with the girls from the medical department. Jean Moyer, the Med Tec, has become a close longtime friend.

In 1958 we purchased a lot in North Lake, Illinois, planning to build a home on it. That did not work out, but in September, 1959 we purchased my Uncle Joe's and Aunt El's home on Wilke Road in Rolling Meadows, Illinois, a community of "starter" homes for first-time buyers. We paid $16,000 dollars for our first house and lived there for seven years.

~

Just before October 24, 1959, when our first child Dawn Marie was born, we stayed at my parents' home in Chicago because it was closer to Swedish Covenant Hospital in case we needed to make a quick trip there. We slept in my parents' bed because it had an electric blanket. All night I kept throwing off the blanket and turning down the heat control. The next morning Lura complained that she did not get a good night's sleep because she was cold and kept turning up the heat control. You guessed it; my parents had the controls reversed.

When Lura was in labor she kept telling the nurse the baby was coming, but the nurse procrastinated in calling the doctor because he was at a party at the country club. When the nurse finally checked Lura, she ran off to call the doctor. Fortunately, another doctor was there who Lura knew and trusted to handle the delivery. At the last minute her doctor arrived just in time to catch the baby. He was not there when he was needed but arrived just in time to collect his fee. Dawn was almost the perfect baby, very content and a wonderful sleeper, so she did not interrupt our life-style much, unlike most couples who experience an abrupt change when their first child arrives.

CUMBERLAND CHURCH

When we moved to the growing Chicago suburb Rolling Meadows we joined the Cumberland Baptist Church, a newly "planted" church that met in a home. We were members 42 and 43. In a small church there are more jobs than people so we both got involved in leadership positions. As a church in a growing suburb of Chicago there were a number of young couples that we made lasting friendships with: Tom and Marlene Warden, Carl and Dolores Sahlin, Al and Vivian McKay and Pastor Frank and Ginny Doten. In 2006 we attended the 50th anniversary of the church where we renewed old friendships.

On May 24, 1960, our son Bill was born at the Arlington Heights Hospital. Bill was a real boy, and unlike Dawn, made a drastic change in our lifestyle. When shopping, Lura had to keep him on a leash because otherwise he would just disappear. Our pastor's wife, Eleanor Fischer, thought this was a bit too drastic, but later she would ask to borrow the leash when she birthed a very energetic child. One Sunday after church I came home to find Lura and Dawn but no Bill. Just then we received a phone call from church; we had left him behind. That was a lack of communication! Lura knew just how Bill felt because as a child she was also left behind at church. During these years I was driving 25 miles each way to work and left Lura home with two children from 7 a.m.to 6 p.m.. She told me she often felt she needed to see a shrink. Fortunately, good neighbors and friends helped make the days more pleasant.

THE WARDEN FAMILY

During the years at Cumberland Church we became very close friends with Tom and Marlene Warden. On weekends we would spend time together, with Lura and

During the years at Cumberland Church, the Wardens, Tom and Marlene (at left) became very close friends.

Marlene enjoying talking, our children playing, and Tom and I in deep discussion about our careers, church and politics. At age 39 Tom was diagnosed with colon cancer and underwent surgery. His doctor assured him that they had gotten all the cancer but recommended chemo as insurance. The doctor either held back from telling Tom what he really knew – a not uncommon practice in those days – or he simply was wrong. Unfortunately, cancer returned and Tom died in 1975 at the age of 41.

"The doctor just told me I have a very short horizon, and I have not done the things that I always really wanted to accomplish." These were the words of a man dying with colon cancer as he lay on his death bed. Tom had confided in me because we were the very best friends and our families were close. What shocked me was that Tom seemed to have it all together; a wonderful wife, four darling children, a home, a career as superintendent of a school district and a dog named Tompta. His words would be my inspiration for the rest of my life. I resolved that every day the Lord gave me I would work to accomplish the things that are the most significant. It was a defining moment in my life. When Tom died he left Marlene with four children ages 16, 14, 8, and 4. His death would have a heavy emotional impact on the children. Why would God allow their father to die just when they needed him most?

Marlene was very concerned about their finances, so on the first Sunday afternoon after the funeral I asked her to bring me all of their financial records. The dining room table was piled high with documents. I spent all afternoon sorting them out and recording their assets and liabilities. When I finished she asked me what her financial situation was and I responded with, "You can make it." But I knew that she was in a very difficult dilemma. There seemed little hope that they could stay in their home.

The Lord gives special care for widows and orphans and he was about to do it for this family. The first thing He did was to supply a job for Marlene as a teacher's assistant. Then, she enrolled in college to earn the credits she needed to obtain her teaching certificate. After two years God led again and she became a fifth grade teacher with an adequate income and benefits for the family. This happened at a time when teaching jobs were hard to find. After impacting the lives of hundreds of children in a career that would last eighteen years, she retired and accepted a position with Media Associates, International. Over the years finances were a constant concern but God provided for her special needs through her church and friends. One Saturday morning an army of men from the church arrived at her house armed with hammers, nails and shingles to re-roof her home. Marlene protected her home, like a mother goose protects her nest, by always making the mortgage payments and providing a stable place for the children to grow up. This would turn out to be a wise decision. There were disappointments along the way.

When her father-in-law died, I called his attorney to
find out how much Marlene would inherit. He informed
me the entire estate had been left to the surviving son,
leaving nothing to his widowed daughter-in-law with
four children. Marlene gracefully accepted his decision
but it troubled me.

After eighteen years of teaching Marlene had enough
service credits to take a "buy-out" retirement with a
pension that provided a base income. For the next five
years she enjoyed working for a mission organization.
Then God provided again in the sale of her home. She
sold at the market peak with the sale price a record for the
community. She also sold it to a neighbor, so there was no
sales commission. The proceeds were used to retire the
balance on the mortgage, buy a condo debt free and
have an investment fund to produce a monthly income.
Today she lives comfortably, volunteers at church and
at a mission organization, travels, has a good relationship
with her four well-adjusted children and enjoys her new
grandchild, Nadia.

After living in Rolling Meadows for seven years,
we bought a home at 210 South Edwards Street in Mt.
Prospect. We wanted more space and to be closer to church
and we were also planning for our third child, Carla,
who would bring great joy into our lives. It was a well-
constructed home with brick exterior, plaster walls and
hardwood floors. We called it "Retirement Villa" because
we planned on living there for a long time. But God had
other plans for us. Eighteen months later, in August of
1966, we moved to Rockford, Illinois. Lura was eight
months pregnant, and on September 10, Carla was born
at the Rockford Memorial Hospital. We did not miss a step
in our lives when Dawn was born, hardly ever missed a
step when Bill was born, but the third child changed our
lifestyle. It would be a year before we started attending
Temple Baptist Church where we would actively serve
for twenty-eight years.

Family Life
CHAPTER III

Mid-life Years in Rockford
.... as I Remember Them

*"For I know the plans that I have for you",
declares the Lord. "Plans for welfare and not
for calamity to give you a future and a hope.
Then you will call upon Me and come and pray
to Me, and I will listen to you. You will seek
Me and find Me when you search for Me
with all your heart."*
– Jeremiah 29:11 - 13

In August 1966, we packed up and moved to 1505 Homewood Drive in Rockford, Illinois, and it turned out to be a defining moment in our lives. Over 36 years in Rockford we would raise our family and experience a full and fruitful life of friendships, church life, ministry, travel, careers and business.

~

ROCKFORD

The need for a move was prompted by a loss of momentum in my career at Bell & Howell. A new Controller was brought into the company from the outside and he brought his team with him. I was not part of the inner circle and did not know how I stood with him. After nine years with the company I was faced with the decision to be content with the situation or move on. I decided to move on and contacted a head-hunter who presented me

with job opportunities from all over the country except the
Chicago area. Finally he found just the right job for me in
Rockford with National Lock Company which interested
us because we had visited a couple of times and liked the
city. Rockford was a medium-size city of 300,000 only 75
miles from Chicago. How I got the job offer is a "God
Thing" I will cover in *My Business Career, Chapter VII.*

With Lura being eight months pregnant when we
moved and with Carla's birth the next month, we waited
a while before looking for the right church. A church just
down the street appealed to us because it was small and
we knew from our Cumberland experience we would be
needed, but we saw some unhealthy things there so started
attending Temple Baptist Church. This was a wise decision
because the church had an active youth program and an
outstanding youth pastor, Greg Speck, who would have a
life-shaping influence on our children and would go on to
be an international youth speaker.

∞

It was the late 60's and early 70's, a period which was
probably the most difficult time in the history of the U.S.
to raise children. It was a wretched time when kids were
told, "Never trust anyone over age 30." It was the "Age Of
Aquarius, the "Hippy" generation and with the unpopular
Vietnam War, cries of "Make Peace, Not War." There was
Supreme Court's Roe vs. Wade decision nullifying the
anti-abortion laws of 38 states permitting 40 million
children to be killed.

Also, there was the Watergate scandal and the resignation of President Nixon; forced school busing; "If it Feels
good, Do It" in regard to sex, drugs and alcohol; the
cultural rebellion of Woodstock and The Beatles and rock
music. The assassinations of President Jack Kennedy,
Robert Kennedy and Reverend Martin Luther King had
us all wondering what had gone wrong with our county.

It was a time when Feminism (man haters who relegated men to clueless creatures and mere sperm banks, so men just dropped out of leadership), and Environmentalism (all development is bad; a caveman mentality) became politically correct. The 1970 movie Love Story showed the chasm between generations.

We were fortunate that God's hand was guiding us and protecting our children. There were many parents who were not as fortunate, like my boss at National Lock. They were a good family, but one of their children rebelled. In high school he would sleep through his classes but would always pass the tests. He would not attend his graduation ceremony to show his contempt for the system. His father visited him at a college in California where he found his son sharing an apartment, without furniture, with a number of students. When he asked his son why was he living in such conditions, the son replied that was all he could afford being on welfare. "With all the wealth our family has, why are you on welfare," his father asked. "It's your system," was his son's reply. Just a few months later his son unsuccessfully tried suicide by shooting himself. After therapy he regained a normal life and went on to marry, have a family and become a successful businessman, but there was a lot of unnecessary pain and hurt. The country that was poised for greatness lost an entire generation because of the loss of family values.

TEMPLE CHURCH

Shortly after we started going to Temple Church, the leadership there learned of my position at National Lock and my financial acumen, so I was invited to a meeting of church leaders, including Pastor Chris Christianson. As the meeting started, a list of seriously past due bills was passed around the room. They all congratulated each other that the

list was down to $30,000. I innocently commented that it
did not look good to me.

They all started to agree with me that it was a real
problem when Pastor Chris jumped to his feet and raised
his voice saying, "Well, if you don't like the way I do
things, I will just leave the meeting," and started to walk
out. Everyone quickly sensed that his feelings had been
hurt and told him to sit down so the matter could be
discussed openly. Being new to the church I had innocently
stepped on a landmine. Pastor Chris was, out of necessity,
personally handling the church's finances.

As you might expect, I was assigned to look into the
situation. The church bookkeeper told me that I just didn't
understand because the problem was that there was not
enough money.

From my past experience in finance I quickly determined that the church accounting system was useless
for controlling expenditures. I structured a budget system
which set cost levels below the current income and adjust-
ed for seasonal giving. Next, I assigned each line item to
one of the church boards. There was confusion because
some of the items were claimed by two boards and
there were others where no one felt accountable. Once
responsibility was established, the problem was solved.

After a few months under the new system the church
was carrying a positive cash balance, all bills were current,
the boards had more clarity about their mission, the bookkeeper no longer had to spend hours juggling the payments
and Pastor Chris, relieved of the financial stress, could
focus on ministry. Thirty years later they were still using
my system.

One of the reasons we decided on Temple was Pastor
Christianson who was a motivating preacher and a good
leader. He had been a B24 bomber pilot during World War
II and his sermons were full of war stories like the time
they just made it back to England with most of the tail
section blasted off his plane by anti-aircraft fire.

I gave Pastor Chris an article by General Electric about strategy which told the story of our government's strategy used to win World War II.

It all started with a small group of men being locked in a Washington, D.C., hotel room and not allowed to leave until they had the mission and basic strategy for the war defined. The strategy group shaped up the plan:for winning the war:

- Total unconditional surrender.
- Give priority to winning the war in Europe first. Save England and use it as the base to invade Europe by eliminating the German submarine force so ships could deliver materials and troops.
- Use strategic air superiority to bomb their industrial capacity that produced war materials (ball bearing and refineries) and to de-moralize the civilian population.
- Capture Europe by invasion from England.
- After winning in Europe transfer resources to Win the war with Japan.

After Pastor Chris read the article he said, "Now I understand why our first priority was bombing the German submarine pens." Pastor Chris was a good leader and moved the church to the growing edge of town where it prospered for many years.

∽

Throughout our 28 years at Temple Lura and I served in many leadership positions. Lura served as leader of the Women's Ministry and headed up the Nursery, Pre-school Sunday School Department, and wedding committee just to name a few. I served on the Finance Committee, Deacon Board, and Elder Board and as Vice Chairman of the Church, just to name a few.

There were two things that we did at Temple which had a lasting impact on our lives and the lives of others. The first was starting a "small group."

During the 1970's and 80's the concept of a Small

Group was just beginning to develop across the country. Willow Creek church in Barrington, Illinois, was at the cutting edge and Lura went there for training. Willow Creek would become a church of small groups, rather than a church with small groups, with 17,000 enrolled in their groups. The operation of a small group is not rocket science but if you do not incorporate four key principles into them they will likely fail. First you need a purpose: service, Bible study, prayer group, social or relational. Defining the purpose will drive the material and the format. Next, you need people who will make the meetings a priority. Poor attendance kills the sense of community needed to bond the group. Next you need a group of 8 to 12 people. It takes a least 8 to have the variety and cross-fertilization necessary for group dynamics. After 12, the small group becomes a class, teacher/student, rather than sharing, and loses it intimacy. Finally, you need individuals who can keep a confidence so bonding can take place. People need to free completely free to express even private things. Once the mechanics are in place you can design the other factors to fit the group – materials, time and place of the meetings and the format that completes the bonding process.

Armed with this information we approached the Assistant Pastor, Lowell Bakke, about starting a small group. He and his wife Diane joined and remained in the group until they were called to another church. The group was successful in bonding us with others in the church and continued for a number of years although membership did change as people moved out of town and were replaced. This good experience would be very useful in future years.

After Pastor Chris left, Reverend Gordon Hanstad was called to the church and would serve for 15 years. Pastor Hanstad had a pastor's heart, the gift of mercy which was what the church needed at that time. He was so gifted in the way he related to people he acted as Police Chaplain and was called upon to tell people that their close relative had been seriously injured or had died.

After repeated efforts to re-direct the church to become

an outreach culture, we decided that it was not our job to change the church because that was the way most people wanted it to be. After 28 years we left the church in good standing with a lot of good friends. Many of our close friends did not understand why we left and assumed we left because of hurt feelings but this was not the case

TEMPLE CHURCH'S HERITAGE

Temple was a great church because it served as an incubator for many people who would go on to impact the world. This church in the Midwest planted and is now reaping what was sown. God used ordinary people, with all

---

The far-reaching impact of Temple Church:

Among the Church's Pastors
5 Became senior pastors
3 Founded their own para-church organization and became internationally known speakers and writers
3 Continued a ministry in music

From 50 Core Lay Families
33 Became pastors or pastors' wives
30 Became missionaries
10 Became leaders in para-church organizations
8 Became lawyers, doctors, counselors, health professionals or were married to one
7 Became philanthropists
10 Became community leaders
11 Became entrepreneurs or senior executives of companies
22 Became church leaders.

their warts, to accomplish extra-ordinary things for his
kingdom. Its role in God's plan was for it to be a "Sending
Church." The church reached its zenith in the mid 1970's
with a membership of 800 but has struggled since then.
The extraordinary thing is that, by my analysis, the people
of this modest-sized church in a modest-sized Midwestern
city have directly or indirectly impacted 100 million
people, and, with the ripple effect, 1 billion people over
the last 40 years.

~

THE LAOTIANS

Another significant thing that Lura and I did at
Temple was to start assisting Laotian refugees to settle in
Rockford. Dr. Larry Edwards challenged us in a Sunday
School class to reach out to Laotians who were just start-
ing to come to Rockford after the fall of Saigon. It would
be a defining moment in our lives.

I remember the arrival on October 6, 1980, of the first
family of six: Kampan Phommachanh (31), the husband;
Lao (29), his wife; Malay (11), Lao's sister; Somphou (7),
Kampan's daughter; and their children Vinay (3) and
Bunny (1).

After a midnight escape from Laos by boat over the
Mekong River with bandits all around, they would spend
the next two years waiting for entry into the U.S. in a Thai
refugee camp. Their dream of coming to America was realized as we picked them up at O'Hare Airport and brought
them to Rockford where they spent the first night with an
established Lao family. Next we moved them into their
apartment, showing them how to adjust the thermostat, use
a vacuum cleaner, use the mail box, etc. We established
some ground rules: They would stay in the apartment we
provided for at least one year, they would stay in Rockford

for at least two years, they would learn English first, then go to work, they would not use welfare (although I had to argue with a social worker over this point because the church would take care of all their needs).

Later these rules proved wiser than we realized because they were necessary for their long term success in blending into the American culture. Then there was the first time we used a bank. I was driving with Kampam in the front passenger seat. I pulled up in the drive-through at the pneumatic depository and asked him for his first paycheck. I placed it in the tube and it was gone. He looked at me in dismay and asked, "Will it come back?" He did not realize it was connected underground to the bank office.

I remember how thrilled Kampam's family was, experiencing their first Halloween where they carved their first pumpkin, having their first sandwich and experiencing their first Christmas, because Laos is an underdeveloped and Buddhist country.

The family came to the U.S. in early October and in late October we all changed our clocks back one hour from Daylight Saving Time to Standard Time. We explained this to them but on Sunday morning they called our house wondering why we had not come to take them to church. We explained again, but on Monday morning the children came back home from school crying because no one was there. When Lura tried to explain it for the third time Kumpunhan, just shook his head and said you change the clock. It never occurred to us that they had lived in a country on the equator where all the days are the same length, so changing the clocks made no sense to them. You can hardly imagine how difficult it is to adjust from a primitive jungle country to the most advanced culture in the world, but they did it, becoming self- sufficient in a mere three months, a record according to one government official.

"Come quickly, he already cold," were the words of a Laotian friend over the telephone one Saturday morning in 1985. Lura and I arrived at their small white bungalow home and found Sysomphone Duangphetmorrakot's corpse lying on the living room floor. As we entered the house, his wife Bounphane frantically threw her arms around me, in total disregard for Laotian custom not to touch a man.

While we where waiting for the Coroner, I tried to tactfully explain what an autopsy was. The Funeral Director was frustrated trying to find out his birthday and relatives. Laotians don't know their exact birth date and have dozens of relatives. Prior to the burial there was a noisy all-night vigil at the house to keep the spirits out. The Buddhist monks had also put a string around the house to keep the spirits out.

When we went to the funeral home to make arrangements, my Laotian friend asked to see the corpse. He wanted to make sure he was really dead and then said, "If my brother, a witchdoctor, were here, he would bring him back to life."

The Laotian burial custom is for each person present to put one shovel full of dirt on the recessed coffin, which was a very emotional experience. Bounphane was unable to do this without help. After the burial I returned to the gravesite. Why had God brought this man half way around the world only to let him die before we could tell him about Jesus?

As I drove out of the cemetery there was a vivid rainbow in the sky although there was no sign of rain. I took it as a sign of God's providence. Sysomphone and Bounphane were the second family we helped settle, so we had the system in place. Lura and I were the leaders but there were many families that demonstrated the compelling love of Christ in practical ways to people that they were not comfortable with Asians, foreigners and Buddhists. One family would be responsible for finding housing – negotiating with the landlord, setting up utilities, pest control, how to adjust the thermostat and how to plunge a backed-up toilet. Another family took care of clothing – making sure each member of the family had adequate clothing for the cold Midwest winter. Education was

Party at Temple Church for Laotians in winter of 1981.

another family's responsibility - registering the children
in school and enrolling adults in English as a Second
Language (ESL). Another family handled employment –
finding a job and arranging transportation.

Another big responsibility was finance – teaching them
all the details of banking like setting up a checking
account, how to make deposits, write checks and live on a
budget. Family medical needs kept another family busy –
doctor visits, birth control, and purging parasites from
their intestinal tracts. Last but not least another family
handled getting them settled in their home – furniture,
dishes, curtains, and bedding.

Every Laotian family had their own harrowing escape
story and Oudone and Sompeng Thirakoune were no
exception. When the Communists took control of their
small village, Oudone was immediately targeted because
he was an educated school teacher, a threat to their
mindless ideology. He was put under house arrest and
scheduled for trial the next day. Under cover of darkness
he escaped and rendezvoused with wife and others in the
nearby jungle, then began the long trek to the Thai border
and freedom. The jungle trail was infested with poisonous
snakes and when one of the children was bitten the child
had to be left behind because his crying would give them

away. What a terrible price a mother would have to pay
for freedom, but there was no choice. When they finally
reached the Mekong River they were ambushed by soldiers
and had to scatter for their lives.

∽

After years in a Thai refugee camp, they arrived in
Carbondale, Illinois, only to be stripped by their sponsors
of their U.S. government grant and left to care for themselves. As with most subcultures, word travels fast, and
they soon learned of our Rockford program that welcomed
refugees.

Oudone was an educated man and was struck by the
difference between Christianity and Buddhism, but after
three years of study was still undecided. Oudone's wife
Sompeng was severely depressed and suffered from
multiple physical and emotional problems. Lura and other
women from the church cared for her, having Bible studies,
prayer times and numerous trips to the doctor. Oudone
realized that these Christian women loved his wife more
than he did, and that was the impetus that made him decide
to become a believer. After three years of teaching without
results, it was the love those women showed his wife that
won his heart. A few years later I asked Sompeng how her
health was and she said, "All my problems just went away
once I had Jesus in my heart.

Oudone was a natural teacher and leader with a
caring heart for his people and he wanted to be a pastor.
He needed to be trained so we approached Moody Bible
Institute. They would not accept him because of a divorce
from his first wife back in Laos, years before he became a
Christian! Then I asked our pastor to take Oudone on as an
apprentice and just let him follow him around for a few
months so he could observe what a pastor does.
Unfortunately, he was unwilling to do this. We finally got

him into a Christian Missionary and Alliance school in a nearby city. He now pastors three Laotian churches near Atlanta, Georgia. Church attendance was voluntary, but most Laotians came because they felt welcome and wanted the events to mingle with Americans. Before Oudone was a believer there was not a single Laotian Christian in the city, so I had to teach Sunday School with Oudone as the interpreter. He was brought up in a Buddhist monastery. He confided to me later that he translated what I said but would add that they could believe it if they wanted. After teaching for three years without a single one coming to Christ, I noticed that my interpreter was adding to what I was teaching. He had become a believer and could now validate what I was teaching. As a result, many Laotians, left their deep Buddhist tradition and accepted Christ. Eventually so many Laotians became believers that they started their own church with an attendance of about 150. In 2008 they built a big new one million dollar church to accommodate 300 people.

The widowed Bounphane was one of the new Laotian believers. Bounphane would again experience tragedy when her second husband divorced her and again when her third husband became a quadriplegic as the result of an automobile accident. He would add to her grief when he died in her arms a few years later. But her faith would see her through it all. She returned to Laos to lead her father to Christ just before he died. She would like to return to Laos as a missionary. She is active in her church and deeply loves Jesus.

Every time I see a rainbow I think about God's providence with the abundant life he has given Bounphane and so many other Laotians.

It was very moving to see how God changed people when we demonstrated his love to Laotian refugees. They experienced repeated tyranny under communism but who found a wonderful life in Christ and in America through the efforts of caring Christians who loved them into the kingdom.

RIVER VALLEY CHURCH

River Valley Community Church was a true "Seeker Church" which appealed to us after our Temple experience. It was a start-up church that was following the Willow Creek model. Not many people knew what a Seeker Church was so this led to a lot of misunderstandings, turnover and turbulence. In the six years we attended about 1,000 people came and left. I know this because I tracked them. Over the ten year history of the church six pastors tried to lead but they were all young and lacked experienced in church planting and could not get things under control. Because the church lacked the core base of mature Christian families and had no roots to establish how things should be done, it was like a ship without a rudder with the engine running at full speed.

Because we both felt the Lord called us to River Valley we assumed leadership responsibilities. Lura headed the Small Group Ministry and I became an Elder. Lura soon became frustrated with the leadership but stayed on the job for several years. Being an Elder was an extremely stressful responsibility and may have contributed to the pastor undergoing intestinal surgery. The stress may have hastened my need for a coronary bypass. I had never encountered so many angry, frustrated and dysfunctional people.

∽

Our Small Group was an enjoyable and rewarding experience. We had a couple in our group who were direct opposites, the wife a very talkative extrovert and the husband a very quite engineering type. During the years we spent together he became a believer and she remarkably matured spiritually. The defining event was when we asked them to have our Small Group meeting at their home. It was the custom for the wife to act as hostess and the husband to lead the discussion. We feared she would take over the meeting, but much to our astonishment she did not interfere and he did an outstanding job. They credited our group with saving their marriage and when they moved to Colorado they remained committed to the Lord. It once again proved the value of Small Groups.

ᕬ

The church met in a public school which required a set-up and tear-down at every Sunday service. It also meant there was no meeting place during the week for teaching the new believers. The "Seeker mode" calls for a Sunday service of excellent quality and with a life application message but no spiritual meat. In an effort to solve the problem, we approached every evangelical church for the use of their facilities during the week but every one rebuffed us. It was very disappointing to see how self-centered churches can be and how they lacked a "Kingdom" mentality. If the church was to go forward it had to have a permanent place to meet.

Our first attempt was to contact a local restaurant that was rumored to be closing and we could offer them a way out. They told us no, but subsequently did go under, and a competing church stepped in and bought it which worked out fine for them. Next we were offered a large parcel of land that was ideally located. Two brothers who owned it offered a bargain price. But then we spent two years waiting for one of the brothers to make up his mind. We finally gave up and the land was subsequently sold to a large corporation. The congregation began to lose confidence in the leadership because each time we convinced them it was a good opportunity they were let down. The next opportunity was a large store building that was available near the Cherry Vale Mall. Once we made an offer a developer exercised an option he had on the building. We had no knowledge of the option and pleaded with him not to exercise it, but to no avail. Again the congregation was disappointed but just then a small shopping center became available. Again we got people involved in how to convert a mall into useable space for a church. We negotiated a price that was accepted and we put $25,000 down and had the bank financing in place. Everything seemed fine; we even had a party at the mall. During the negotiations we had asked the trustees to have the roof inspected. I had urged them to use Carlson Roofing Company. Larry Carlson was a client of mine and I knew he was competent to do the inspection, but they had another company do it. That company stalled, not giving us a final evaluation. Then it came out that a new roof was needed and it would cost $250,000. We tried to re-negotiate the deal but to no avail. That killed the deal and we lost our $25,000.

By this time the congregation thought the leadership was totally inept and all credibility was lost, so when the next opportunity came along we decided to keep it secret. It was a stand-alone theater at the Cherry Vale Mall that was closed. The first step was to have zoned by the City of Cherry Valley. When the proposal came before the city council, it became known to the local newspaper, the Rockford Register Newspaper which called the church office to get the story. We pleaded with them not to print the story but they said the information was in the public domain and they were going to print it. We had no choice but to reveal our secret. Once again we got people involved in how to convert a theater into usable church space. The acquisition was ready to go, except that Sears, as a mall anchor store, had to approve it. Despite all our efforts, they stalled for over six months and the deal collapsed.

It was clear to everyone that it was not God's timing or that Satan did not want the church to exist. The pastor left, we left and so did a number of others. Despite all the problems and disappointments we saw more people come to faith in Christ in six years at River Valley than we saw at Temple in twenty-eight years. But here is the rest of the story.

A small group decided not to bail out. One Sunday morning a man drove by the school where services were

in session and noticed the portable sign in front of the
school advertising River Valley Community Church.
He said to himself, "Now there is a church that needs a
building, and I think I will give them one." He offered
several sites, lease payments of $1 a year for 10 years,
an option to buy and $10,000 to help remodel the building.
    The church moved into a new facility in a good
location, and has grown ever since as Rockford's only
true "Seeker Church." On a return visit we found lots
of happy people. God's timing is always best and the
outcome made it all worth while.

$$\sim$$

OUR CHILDREN

Dawn was a very compliant and happy child,
a phlegmatic. When we moved to Rockford she was able
to just coast for the first semester of second grade because
the Rockford school system was about that far behind the
Mt. Prospect system. She did well in grade school because
the school principal was a Christian who was competent
and hired good teachers. She enjoyed church activities
and even joined the local Brownie Club. There was some
sibling rivalry with Bill. He was told never to hit a girl,
a good life principle, but one time Lura sensed that things
were too quiet and looked into the next room to see the
two of them pounding each other. They were keeping quiet
because they knew they were not supposed to fight. One
time Dawn asked what her I.Q. score was, and I told her
she was better off not knowing, but she persisted. I finally
told her, and then she wanted to know my score. It was
one of the few times in my whole life I would deliberately
lie. I told her my score was two points higher than hers.
    In 1973 we moved from Homewood Drive to
Flossmoor Court for two reasons. The first was to change
schools for the kids and the second was to provide each of

The Lawrenz family. Front from left: Carla and Brynn Maria, Lura and Bob. In the back from left are the Sjolunds: Paul, Kiersten, Shari Joy, Dawn, and Marie Nicole. Bill and Yasuko are on the right.

our children with their own bedroom. Each child having their own space promotes better family life because they can always have the option of retreating into their private area of the house.

During Dawn's teen years there were church choir trips which were a great experience and time for group bonding. At Guildford High School she was on the academic fast track and became a National Scholarship Finalist. By her senior year Dawn was ready for college, both academically and relationally. We visited several colleges, but Bethel University in St. Paul, Minnesota was her choice. Those ready to enter college seem to instinctively know which college is the right one just by visiting the campus. I remember visiting the college and asking about the S.A.T. scores of entering freshmen. The representative of the college tactfully asked if I was concerned that Dawn's score was too low. I responded that my concern was that it was too high and that Bethel would not be challenging enough for her. When we arrived at Bethel, I told Dawn all the money allotted for the first year was in her checking account. She asked what would happen if it was not enough. I told her that she had a choice of working or going hungry When the school year ended we went to Bethel to pick her up. As we were about to leave she remembered she had to pay her final bill. She came back and reported she had $12.22 left.

❦

At Bethel Dawn met Paul Sjolund who was 100 percent Swedish. Rockford was 50% Swedish, so we had lots of Swedish friends, and I loved to tell Swedish jokes. My friends had a wonderful time getting back at me when Paul Sjolund married Dawn in August of 1980 and gave me three Swedish grandchildren. Our friends George and Phyllis Carlson gave us a Swedish party just for fun.

Paul and Dawn's wedding was a heartwarming time. When Paul asked us for our blessing on their marriage, we told them we had only one reservation, and that was that they both continue their education and graduate. I had little concern because it was evident Paul deeply loved Dawn. There was a dinner party at the Clock Tower Inn and they were married at Temple Baptist Church.

It was a struggle for a few years as Paul went full time to the University of Minnesota to earn a degree in Mechanical Engineering and worked part-time, and Dawn worked full time and went part-time to the University to earn a Degree in Business Administration. Once school was complete, Paul worked for Honeywell and Dawn

worked for the State of Minnesota Department of
Revenue. Then they bought their first home and attended
Salem Baptist Church in New Brighton, a St. Paul suburb.
In 1986 Marie Nicole our first grandchild arrived, then
Shari Joy in 1989, and Kiersten in 1995. In 1983 they
bought their first home and sold it in 1988, moving to the
Champlin, Minnesota, to plant a new church, Grace
Fellowship. It showed their commitment to the Lord
of their lives. I remember going to their first public
service in a school with about 250 people. In a few years
the church purchased seventeen acres of land and built
a building with three additions totaling 80,000 square feet.
Attendance is now over 1,000 people per week. In addition, the church has spawned 17 new church plants, which
means over 10,000 people hear about Christ per week.

   I remember a frantic call from Dawn, "Paul has quit
his job at Honeywell and wants to start his own business.
Can you come up to help?" In one afternoon we put
together a Marketing Plan, Business Plan, the name
Microvision, and the ownership. Paul would own 50 percent. Other than that, they had no product, no customers,
no manufacturing facilities and no money, but they were
in business! It would be five months without a paycheck
before their first order came from Texas Instruments with
a 50 percent advance. It was a defining event because now
they were really in business and it would grow into an
extremely profitable company. Twelve years later they
would sell the business for enough that Paul and Dawn
did not have to work anymore, and they could devote full
time to their family and ministry. Paul served as Elder,
Chairman of the Missions Committee, and Chairman of
the Building Committee and a board member for two
mission organizations, Frontiers and Africa Works. Dawn
home schooled all three children, and was administrator
for the church home school group, just a few of the many
responsibilities she had.

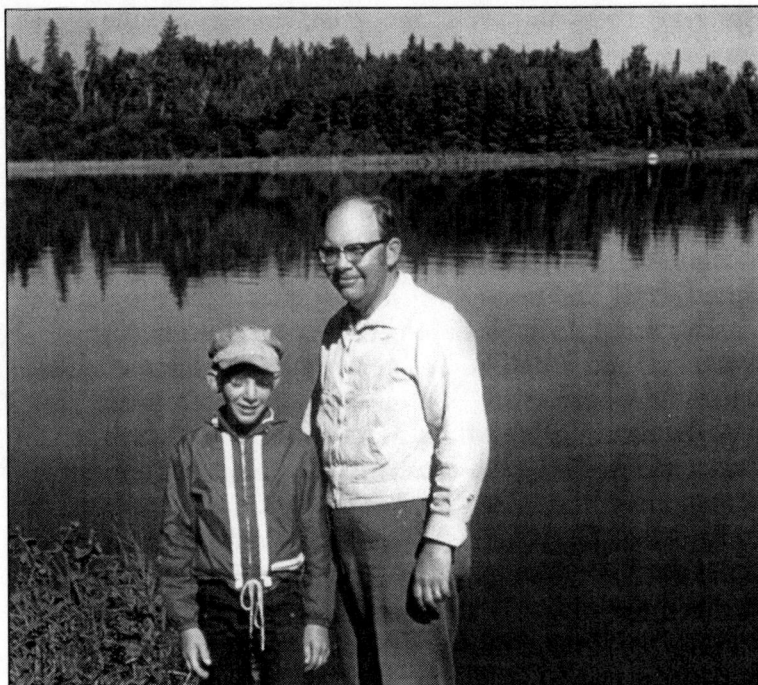

**A great time together with son Bill in 1975
at Lac de Mille Lake in Ontario, Canada.**

      **Bill was an extremely active child, very likable and
gifted in relating to adults,** a true sanguine. He was the
kind of boy who would grow vegetables in his garden,
harvest them, place them in his wagon and go door-to-door
selling them. He also had a good business representing
the Brown Greeting Card Company. Bill was active at
Temple in the boys' club and made small cars to race on
a track. One year he won the competition. We still have
those cars. In his teen years he was active in the youth
program where Youth Pastor Greg Speck had a great
influence on him. For many years Bill and I, with some
friends, would go to Lac de Mille Lake in Canada fishing
and camping while Lura and the girls would go on a
shopping spree. We had a great time tent camping,

drinking water directly from the lake and eating the fish we caught. On one occasion, Bill took all the boys off into the woods and got lost. Some of the fathers were concerned when the boys did not return, but I was confident because he was experienced in wilderness survival, and besides, I knew we were on an island so they could not go very far. Bill and I also went to the Boundary Waters on the Minnesota-Canadian boarder and had a great time fishing and portaging our canoe from lake to lake.

Bill had a difficult time in school until we had him evaluated and found he had a hearing-and-vision condition which he would eventually outgrow. His sixth grade year was the most difficult because the class was always in chaos and he could not concentrate. I knew the middle school environment would destroy him, so we enrolled him in Rockford Christian School which was a defining event. After the first grading period, he told me he wanted to be on the honor roll. My first reaction was setting high goals was a good thing, but my second thought was, it was unrealistic and he would be disappointed. But he had two teachers who took an interest in him and he excelled, graduating with honors. He was confident and ready when he entered Guildford High School.

One day Bill and I were sailing my boat on Rock Lake. It was a 12 foot Butterfly sailboat, the USS PATIO, with a dagger board protruded below the hull. When we sailed around a point of land, the dagger board caught the lines of a fisherman who became very angry. I sailed toward shore to apologize and compensate the man who by this time was cursing at us. While I planned on handling the situation, Bill said he wanted to talk with the man. I agreed and Bill was very respectful and charmed him to the point where he apologized to us and refused compensation. Bill graduated from Guildford, spent two years at Rock Valley College and then three years at Seattle Pacific University where he earned a double degree in Psychology and Communications.

Bill loved Seattle and spent a year there looking for

employment, but it was before Reagan Economics kicked in, and he could not find a job. During this time Bill developed an interest in the Japanese and attended a Japanese-American church. He went to Japan one summer to teach English and found it a rewarding experience and was interested in returning. I remember discussing the situation over with him when he came home for Christmas. I advised him to set a date and if nothing developed by the date, jump on a plane and go to Japan and look for a job. The day before the target date he still had no leads but decided to apply for a visa. It was as if God was testing him, because within twenty-four hours he had a plane ticket and a job in Japan. Bill was a tent-maker missionary and would spend the next fifteen years in Japan teaching English at a number of different schools, grade levels and free-lance.

After Bill had lived in Japan for several years, Lura and I flew to Narita Airport in Tokyo and then on to Osaka to visit Bill, who was suppose to meet us at the airport. However, Bill did not show up and left us stranded. We tried to use a telephone to call him but could not figure out how to use the phone. Lura finally convinced someone to place the call for us, and she talked to Bill's roommate who in turn called Bill. Bill thought we were coming a day later. He arrived at the airport in a taxi after it had closed for the night to find us at the curb waiting for him. Bill felt badly about it, but cautioned us not to tell anyone because in the Japanese culture what had happened would be regarded as extremely disrespectful to parents. We had a great time meeting Bill's friends, visiting numerous cities and seeing many interesting things. *See Foreign Travels, Chapter V.*

∽

Bill had always liked Asian women, even during his high school days. In Japan he had a problem. Some women would be attracted to him, but he would ignore them, while other women he was attracted to would not give him any encouragement. One day at the International Church, he saw Yasuko Kanai and was immediately attracted to her, but she was going with another guy. Bill thought to himself that if they would ever break up, he would be interested in her. She did break up with the guy, and Bill got her on the rebound.

After dating Yasuko for a number of months, in January 2000, Bill called us and said he would like to bring Yasuko home to meet us because they wanted to get married. A week later he called again to say they loved each other, had decided to get married while home in the U.S., and could Lura arrange a wedding for them in six weeks. Bill was depending on his mother because she was on the Wedding Committee at Temple Church and knew how to do it. Lura put the wedding together, and it was a memorable time. Because Bill and Yasuko came home just two days before the wedding day, special arrangements were required with the seamstress to fit her wedding dress. Yasuko had a good attitude about Lura's preparations for the wedding because Lura had made all the decisions - time and place of the wedding ceremony, the wedding dress, the colors, flowers, and reception. When Lura would ask her for decisions over the telephone Yasuko would say, "Whatever is least laborious for you."

A dinner for the wedding party and family was held at the Clock Tower Inn where I gave a short talk entitled "Welcome to the Family" and everyone was given the opportunity to say "Welcome to the Family" in a different language. There were about twelve different languages in our extended international family. The wedding took place at the Shiloh Free Church in Rockford with the reception at the Rockford Airport. At the reception, Yasuko's father gave a long speech in Japanese and Yasuko translated it into English. Then Yasuko gave a wonderful talk about how just a few years earlier our two counties were at war and were now at peace.

As a pre-teen Yasuko told her father she wanted to be
an "International Person," so he knew he would lose her at
an early age. Yasuko was a high school exchange student
in the United States and went on to Dartmouth College,
so she became very fluent in English.

After fifteen years in Japan, Bill and Yasuko decided to
move to Hong Kong and teach at a private school. During
time off, they vacation at their second home in Hawaii.

∽

**Carla, a melancholy, was a delight. She loved
children and animals, especially horses.** Lura and I
thought a great deal about having a third child since we
already had a girl and boy. Since Bill was becoming more
controllable and independent, we decided on having a third
child, a decision we would never regret. Carla was born
shortly after we moved to Rockford. We did not have my
parents support for child care, so it took a year to regain
our social life. From a very early age, she was interested
in stories about orphaned children and animals.

By age eight Carla was asking for her own horse, but I
told her she had to pay for it, so she began saving. She was
taking horseback riding lessons and learned all about how
to care for a horse. When she was 10 years old from her
instructor she learned of a horse that was available for
$800. With her life savings she bought Key, a bay, fifteen
hands high. I remember him being delivered to a farm
about five miles from our home. It was summertime and
Carla and her friend Christine would spend entire days at
the farm, riding and grooming Key. However, Key went
lame and after many visits to the vet, Carla decided she
had to sell him to save him from a life of pain. I asked
Carla if she wanted me to handle the disposal of the horse,
and she agreed. On Saturday we went to the farm and said
goodbye to Key. On Sunday it rained, and by Monday
morning it was below freezing. I led Key from the barn
down the driveway to the trailer, but when the horse got on

the driveway he began dancing. He had frozen mud on his hooves and slipped when they were on the hard surface of the driveway. I remember it was very cold, and getting the horse to lift one leg with the other three being unstable was a real challenge. I finally used a hammer and screwdriver to chisel the ice from each hoof. Key got an apple as a farewell gift.

∾

One of the reasons we moved to Flossmoor Court was to change school districts. We moved into the Guilford High School and the Guilford Center Grade School districts - both had good reputations. The grade school was a naturally racially integrated school which was a plus in our thinking because we were concerned about racism in the Rockford culture. However, the school district was under a court order to integrate the entire system, and a large number of minority children were bussed to the school. Mr. Roof, the principal, did not know how to handle the influx of black students and the entire school deteriorated. Mrs. Warren was Carla's third grade teacher who was totally unfit to teach. Carla would come home from school with poor paper marked "A." Mrs. Warren said Carla was one of her best students.

One day I picked Carla up at school and she said that Mrs. Warren must not be a Christian because she hated children. Lura went to see Mrs. Warren and found her classroom in chaos. She went to see the principal, Mr. Roof, and he just made excuses for her, so I went to see him. He was clueless about how to deal with the situation. I gave him the short course on how to handle an incompetent employee in a union situation, but he said I would have to go to the school headquarters because he did not want to face up to the situation. When I met with the superintendent, she pulled Mrs. Warren's file and found not a single evaluation as required by school policy. She said it would take five years to get her removed, so I gave up. We placed Carla in Rockford Christian School the next year, and left Mrs. Warren and Mr. Roof behind. Carla thrived at RCS and went on to Guildford High School, Bethel University, and University of Wisconsin graduate school and then returned to Rockford where she got a job with the Rockford Public School system. Her principal did not even welcome her to the school and slept though meetings. Guess who? Mr. Roof. Meanwhile, Lura was working at Woodward Governor Company and a fellow employee said she did not know what to do because her child had such an incompetent teacher. Guess who? Mrs. Warren. Both were still in the system because the union protected them, but how many children were short-changed in all those years?

∽

Carla was born with cleft cavus deformity (high arch) in her right foot. As a child, I would have to carry her if a walk was too long. The doctors advised us to wait for corrective surgery until she stopped growing, so when she was eighteen we had an orthopedic surgeon perform the surgery. It took about six months for her to recover and everything seemed to be progressing. Then she started having pain. She completed her under-graduate work at Bethel University, with a degree in linguistics and psychology, and went to graduate school at the University of Wisconsin -Eau Claire in the Speech Therapy program. By this time she was in constant pain and taking medications that upset her equilibrium. We had already seen doctors in Rockford, Minneapolis and two visits to the Mayo Clinic.

I began a period of constant prayer. One night she called home to see if she should go to a homeopathic doctor who uses natural medications, recommended by a classmate. She thought if she could discontinue the synthetic medications she was on, it would relieve her vertigo and nausea. We said she could go but just not signup for continuing visits. When she visited the doctor he asked a lot of questions, examined the foot and gave it a forceful crack, a loud pop and he said, "Oh." He instructed her to walk around and there was no pain. "When do I come back?" Carla asked. He said there was no reason for her to return. After dozens of doctor visits, orthopedic shoes, and thousands of dollars, an unknown doctor in an unknown specialty in an unknown town solved her problem. God answers prayer.

After spending nine months in Rockford saving her money, Carla moved back to Minneapolis and began work at Ruben Lindh, a social service agency for preschool disadvantaged children. A few years later she would take a one-year leave of absence and go as a missionary to the Children's Shelter of Cebu, Philippines. Her original assignment was to work with cerebral palsy kids, to teach them how to use a reader board. One of her clients was a CP boy named Jeff who could not talk or express himself. After training him on the reader board, they made a field trip to McDonalds where for the first time in his life he was able to tell what he wanted – hamburger, French fries and a king-sized Coke. What a thrill for Carla. She was soon reassigned to manage the school. Half-way through her year it was Christmas and Paul and Dawn, their three children, Bill and Lura and I visited her. We had a wonderful time: children's Christmas party, staying at two different resorts, sight seeing and encouraging Carla with the responsibilities she had at the school.

❧

As planned, Carla returned to her job at Ruben Lindh to be with the children she loved, and found it very rewarding to help the kids, possibly being their only hope for a productive life. For several years Carla had said that if she was not married by age forty she would adopt a child as a single mom. At age forty she put the process in motion hoping that she would not have to wait too long.

In January, 2008, Lura and I accompanied her to

Here we are at the Central Park Fountain in Antigua, Guatemala, with daughter Carla and granddaughter Brynn Maria. Born in Guatemala, Brynn was adopted by Carla in 2008.

Guatemala. It was a heart-warming experience to be present when the foster mother handed over 7 month old Maria de Los Angeles into Carla's welcoming arms. After the emotional handover from the foster mother in the hotel lobby, Carla finally had her own little girl. It was a dream come true and there seemed to be immediate bonding.

Two days later we took Brynn for her required visit to the American Embassy to obtain a passport. At the Embassy we all spent three long hours waiting in a long line, along with about thirty other families, all with fussing babies.

We spent a few extra days in Guatemala visiting Antigua, the former capitol of Guatemala, that helped us all adjust

to the new family situation. When we were at the
Guatemala airport to return home. it became obvious that
Brynn was sick. Due to an airline glitch Byrnn did not
have her own seat and Carla had to hold her sick child
during the long flight home. We received a royal reception
at the airport in Minneapolis, with Dawn, the girls, and
a host of about dozen friends greeted us with signs and
balloons. Fortunately Carla had arranged to take the next
six weeks off work as she learned to be a mommy and she
and Brynn got acquainted.

We see Brynn often and enjoy seeing the daily changes,
unlike our other three granddaughters who were 350 miles
away when they were growing up that we never got to
see. But the adoption almost did not happen. An international treaty was enacted which was to prevent human
trafficking, but had the effect of ending all international
adoptions from Guatemala. The deadline was December
31, 2007, but U.S. Senator Norm Coleman met with the
President of Guatemala and reached an understanding that
all adoptions is process could continue. Byrnn was one
of the last children to be adopted by a foreigner. She was
spared a life in a state operated orphanage for the first
eighteen years of her life. It was God at work.

Each of our three children has adopted a Christian
world view, exercising their faith in Christ in a practical
and productive lifestyle that allows them to provide for
themselves while caring for others. I give their mother
credit. When my parents became born-again Christians,
they provided a foundation for the next three generations
to experience the transformation that only faith in Christ
can provide.

∾

FAMILY LIFE

We had a good family life with supper time being a
daily get-together. At one point I invented a game whereby

each child was paid $5.00 per day for their school
work - just like dad earned money for his work. Now
that they had an income, they would have to pay for living
expenses; $1.50 per day for rent, $.50 per day for utilities,
$.50 per day for maid service to make their bed and clean
their bedroom, $.25 for breakfast, $.25 for lunch, $.50 for
supper, $.50 per hour to watch TV and $1.00 per week
for taxes. At each supper time I would give each one their
$5.00 and collect for the day's expenses. They decided
that the $.50 per day for their mother's maid service was
a rip-off, so they would do it themselves and save the
money. They also received a discount on their utility
charge if they turned out the lights when leaving a room,
which they started doing. Then, there was the TV charge.
They decided to share the cost by mutually agreeing to
watch one program, which ended the constant bickering
over who got to watch their favorite program. It was a
fun game and a great teaching tool.

One of the kids at the end of the game said, "There is
so little left after all the money I earned." The game was
a total success.

∽

One of the things we did as a family was to go on
a vacation every year. Two vacations are worthy of
note because they were especially great family times.

The first vacation was to Colorado. We rented a
tent-camper and off we went across the Great plains.
I remember when we reached eastern Colorado there was
something on the horizon that looked like dark clouds,
but it turned out to be the magnificent Rocky Mountains.
We visited Denver, the mile high city; Colorado Springs
with its Garden of the Gods and the Air Force Academy;
Pueblo – Great Sands Dunes National Monument, where
we climbed 800 foot sand dunes and slid down on cardboard boxes like a toboggan ride; Durango and the Narrow
gauge Railroad up the mountains to Silverton; Mesa Verde

National Park and the Indian dwellings in the cliffs;
Ouray and a hazardous Jeep drive up the old mining
roads into the mountains where we saw a cougar; Black
Canyon of the Gunnison - just one big hole like the Grand
Canon except narrower. The trip was recommended by
my brother-in-law Ed Kerr and it lived up to our
expectations as a great family vacation.

∽

The second vacation was to Montana and Alberta,
Canada. We drove to Helena, Montana, where we joined
Don and Kathy Pederson and their two sons, Brian and
Jeffery. The plan was for us to tent camp, and they would
rent an RV from Bob's Fine Used Cars to provide cooking
and toilet facilities for all of us. This really appealed to
Kathy and Lura. However, the RV was a disaster. On the
very first day we had trouble flushing the toilet, so Don
gave the lever a hard pump and it broke off which made
it unusable for the rest of the trip. Next, a large mirror fell
off the wall and covered the floor with glass splitters. This
was followed by the doorknob coming off the maintenance
door, which meant we had to climb over the front seat to
enter or leave the vehicle. On several occasions the engine
would not start because the carburetor was not set for high
attitudes. Then, there was the flat tire. Because it was
double rimmed, we could not change it ourselves and
had to be towed into town like a harpooned whale.
    We did not, however, let all these problems dampen
our enjoyment of all the beautiful scenery, seeing
interesting things and having fun. For years afterwards
we joked about Bob's Fine Used Cars.
    The trip began by traveling north through the Rocky
Mountains to Waterton, Alberta, Canada. We thought it
was the most beautiful expanse of water and mountains
in the world and enjoyed swimming a pool enclosed with
glass to protect us from the cool breezes. Further north in

Banff, we took a gondola ride up the mountain to view
the city set in a mountain paradise. Then, on to Lake
Louise with its expanse of peaceful beryl blue water
from the glacier melt. This has to be one of the most
inspirationally beautiful settings on earth. Then we drove
even farther north to the Jasper National Park and the
Columbia Ice Fields. I remember thinking:

"Why go to Switzerland when you can see the same
thing here and avoid the time and cost of transatlantic
air travel. Also, the people speak English and the food
and money is similar to the U.S." We all had a wonderful,
never to be forgotten time. Unfortunately, Carla picked
up salmonella along the way and was very sick all the
way home. We were glad to be traveling with Don
who was a doctor.

$\sim$

OUR DOGS

Every boy and every family needs a dog. As a boy
I had Tippy and Ginger. It was not until we moved to
Rockford that our family had its first dog. We tried cats
but that did not work out. I always tell cat lovers, "I like
cats, they taste just like rabbit!" Dogs brought fun and
enjoyment to our family, at least most of them. Our first
family dog was Shadow, a poodle/terrier who had five
puppies. Shadow was a smart dog. She, like all of our
dogs, was trained to stay in the yard. Our neighbors always
assumed we had an invisible fence, since the dogs would
run to the property line and stop, but we didn't. After eight
years as part of our family it was hard to take her to the
vet for her final ride. I cried.

Our next dog was Daisy, an Airedale Terrier, who was
an escape artist. We would put her in a cage when we left
home, and when we returned home she would be at the
door to greet us. We never did figure out how she got out

of the cage. We tried locking her in the basement, but she tore everything up. After a short time we decided Daisy was not the dog for us and sold her to another family who loved her even though they could not keep her confined either. Dusty, a Schnauzer, was next in line. She had three Schnauzer puppies. One of the puppies was given to Paul and Dawn. Despite being trained to stay in the yard, one night Dusty ran off and was killed by a car. I remember going to the Animal Control office to identify her and cut off her I.D. tag as a remembrance. Rascal was our next dog, but he did not last long. We would have him outside for 30 minutes but as soon as he came in the house he would do his "business." He was incorrigible and chewed up everything. He also was a biter.

"Faithful Black Dog" Jasper was our smartest dog. He was able to play the piano and retrieve the right colored ball on command. (Dogs are color blind, so he must have learned to distinguish the markings on the ball.) He also did math problems, giving the answer by turning around in a circle the correct number of times. He gave us fourteen years of enjoyment but finally died of cancer.

When we moved to Minnesota in 2002, Carla urged us to get a dog for companionship. She found a breeder and we went and agreed on Kobi, who was just a pup. He is our most personable dog and does a lot of tricks – lie down, shake, sit up, fetch and hoop for a Cheerio dipped in cream cheese and Greenies as rewards. He loves to curl around Lura's neck while she is sitting in a chair. If I am still in bed, at 8:00 sharp he will straddle me for a rub and scratch and lick my hand in loving appreciation. He is our first white dog, being a West Highland Terrier and Shiatsu combination. He gives us great enjoyment and is a faithful friend. Carla tells us he is spoiled and she is probably right. All of our dogs were faithful friends who became part of the family and added immensely to our enjoyment of life.

OUR PARENTS

During our time in Rockford both Lura's and my parents relocated there to be close to us. As they grew older they would require more and more time and attention, which put heavy demands on Lura's time. We had committed, as part of our core values, to care for our parents, whatever it took, a virtue I saw in my parents. Both my father and father-in-law were very influential in shaping my life and values.

My father was not only a father, he was a trusted friend, and I still miss him 20 years after his passing. We would spend hours talking about life and how to succeed and have a meaningful life. He taught me the value of acquiring knowledge, just facts about everything; then assembling the facts into how things work and what makes people tick, understanding; and then how to apply them to life, wisdom. I learned about how to plan ahead and the part that savings and investing play in proving the basic foundation for being self- sufficient and then using that base for serving others. By his example, he taught me to be authentic by being consistent in living out my Christian values at home, at work, and at church, which I believe had a strong influence on my children. He taught me by example that life was a continuous learning and growing experience. When he completed grade school his father told him to quit school and go to work to help support the family, so at age 12 he had his first job as an errand boy for a Chicago business. After a few other jobs he began working for the Western Electric Company, which was the equipment supplier for the AT&T phone system. He made himself a valued employee by learning all about the equipment and their numbering system.

When an opportunity came he was transferred to the Illinois Bell Telephone Company because of his specialized knowledge. This was very unusual because the company policy was "no transfers." In the 1930's, the

Three Lawrenz generations – Son Bill, my father Ambrose and I at a get-together in Galena, Ill.

State of Illinois began registration of engineers and he was grandfathered in because he was doing engineering-level work. He had earned a status usually reserved for college graduates with degrees in electrical engineering.

After the age of 50 he became interested in painting. He had always had beautiful handwriting but never thought of it as an artistic talent. It began when he was recovering from major surgery and someone gave him a gift of a paint-by-numbers kit. When the first painting was finished he looked at it and decided he could do a better painting without the numbers. That was the beginning of a 20 year career as an artist which would last until his death in 1984. During those years he probably painted 100 pictures, so our home has a number of his original oils hanging on the walls, a wonderful remembrance of him.

Lura's dad, Fred Alexander, was a minister who always took the hard road and lived very frugally. After meeting his wife (who came from a very affluent Philadelphia family) at Asbury College in Kentucky, he pastored several churches in upstate New York and then moved to Kansas. One of his favorite ministries was operating a Christian Servicemen's Center in Salina, Kansas, both during World War II and then again during the Korean conflict. Fort Riley was close by and literally hundreds of lonely servicemen would come in for good food and fellowship. Ladies from churches in Salina and miles around there brought in wonderful home baked pies, cakes and cookies which made a warm home-like atmosphere. In 1956 they moved to Cleveland, Ohio, where he taught at a Bible School for black students and lived in a ghetto.

When they later moved to Savanna, Ohio, he became the editor and publisher of The Other Side, a magazine devoted to informing evangelical Christians about racial prejudice. Many Christians, like me, have no idea how insidious and sinful racism is. By spending time with him in thoughtful conversation and reading books he recommended, "Black like Me" and "Jubilee", I began to realize

Lura's parents Anne and Fred Alexander. were faithful servants of the Lord in a life of ministry.

what a racist I really was. He and Anne were faithful servants of the Lord all of their lives and God miraculously provided for them. Anne saved by the penny most of their lives, but it was Fred's sister Pearl who provided the funds so they could be cared for at the Fairhaven Retirement Home in Rockford, Illinois. I invested their savings, and at the end of one year, I listed all my client's returns. Fred and Anne's account was at the top of the list with a 36 percent return. God provides for those who serve him unselfishly.

My mother, from a family of 12 children, also shaped my life in profound ways. She had a tender heart which taught me how to look for people's needs and opportunities to help. She was an optimist and a very happy person, typical of the Irish. I inherited this trait and learned to always look for the good and to figure out some way to make things come out right; regardless of how difficult the situation looked. This would be a valuable asset throughout life and in my business. I also acquired her DNA that gave me a healthy body. My father was sick much of his life.

My mother's life span covered almost the entire 20th century. Born in 1904, she lived 94-1/2 of the 100 years. In her lifetime, she lived under the administration of 17

My parents Margaret- and Ambrose Lawrenz. Their strong faith in God was very important in preparing the way for me.

Presidents, starting with Rough Rider President Theodore
Roosevelt, who in 1904 began construction of the Panama
Canal. As a young girl, she watched her father light real
candles on the Christmas tree. The family all sat and
watched as Dad would snuff out each candle as it burned
short. She was impressed by the family doctor, who was
the first person she knew to have a car. As a teenager, she
watched men march off to World War I. She was a flapper
of the 20's where dancing the Charleston was the primary
social event of the week. The Aragon Ballroom was the
place for a Dime-a-Dance with a different neat guy signed
up on your dance card for each dance of the evening.
When she and dad married in 1926, they never went to
those dances again.

After seven years of marriage, I arrived on the scene.
It was Prohibition. They celebrated with beer made in
the bathtub. It was the Depression. Everyone was poor.
Families helped each other, but the Depression made
an indelible impression on all who experienced it.

Then it was Pearl Harbor and World War II. I remember Sunday afternoon, December 7, 1942, when my parents
explained what "war" meant. For the first time my dad
allowed my mother to go to work at the Douglas Aircraft
Company to help win the war. Only recently have histori-
ans realized that it was Marge who was responsible for
feeding the workers who built the planes, which carried the
bombs, that weakened the enemy that enabled the army to
win the war. And you thought it was "Rosy the Riveter"
who made the critical difference in winning! But now you
know "the rest of the story". After the war, she worked at
Marshall Fields and Peterson's Ice Cream Parlor, two
of her favorite places in the whole world. During her life-
time, there was the advent of cars, radio, central heat, air
conditioning, TV, microwaves, jet planes, atomic energy,
space travel, cell phones, computers and talking color
motion pictures. As significant as these economic,
political, scientific and cultural events were, they did not
define my mother. Her life was built around family, friends

and her faith in Jesus Christ. Her perspective on the world was an unusual confidence in herself. From her vantage point, she was like the North Star, a fixed point in time and space, all the world changed but she didn't. In the latter years, she began to get shorter due to osteoporosis. One day, while standing next to her daughter-in-law, Lura, she observed, "Lura, you are getting taller." It never occurred to her that she was the one who was changing.

As the 8th child of 11, born into an Irish Catholic family in Chicago, she knew a lot about family life. As a child, she attended Our Lady of the Angels School. Even though she described the nun teachers as "those devils", she had a life long deep respect for the Catholic Church. She embraced family in good times and difficult times. When her sister-in-law, Molly, died, her children Rich and Gerry became like her own children. She lived longer than any member of the family, including all of their spouses.

As her only child, I could do no wrong; although the threat of a spanking with the hairbrush was sometimes necessary. I married the perfect wife; we had perfect children and then perfect grandchildren. We were "shopped over" and "cooked over" for an endless number of birthdays, anniversaries, holidays, graduations, and countless non-events. She excelled at shopping and cooking. She had endless energy to play with the grandchildren, or shop until the stores closed, and she did it all in high heels. She literally baked thousands of delicious pies. Nothing was too good for us! Even Shadow, the family dog, was given those extra hard, smooth bones from the delicious leg of lamb dinners she would prepare for us.

Her devotion was amazing, as she cared for her husband of 58 years. My dad had major health problems almost all of his adult life. He came close to dying at least three times. Her devoted care kept him alive until 1984. She lived on as a widow for over 14 years. Mom and Dad were such a good match that they slept in the same bed without realizing that the electric blanket controls were switched. Family was the core of her life, but it was surrounded by her faith in Jesus Christ. As a girl, she was given a basic understanding of God and Christ at home, at school and at church. As a young wife and mother, she attended mass regularly. She tells about how, as a young girl, she slipped into a neighborhood tent meeting — complete with sawdust — to hear the great preacher, Peter Deyneka speak on personal faith in Jesus Christ. She never forgot what she experienced that night.

Mother was no theologian, but she knew God, trusted steadfastly in the Lord's faithfulness to deal with anything this life offers and constantly prayed for those around her. Her joyful and upbeat approach to life confirmed her belief that "all things work together for good for those who love God." Her life reflected her faith. She gave generously of herself to those around her. In my whole life, I have never doubted for a minute that my mother loved me, so it was an easy step to understand that God could love me too. She spoke often to people to trust God and pray. In recent years, she said, "Why am I living so long? Why doesn't God take me home?" She had no fear of dying and looked forward to being with the Lord and with her darling husband. She and dad have left a lasting legacy of family, good friends and faith in Jesus Christ.

$$\sim$$

OUR FRIENDS

Another person who helped shape my life was my trusted friend Don Treash. I met Don at the University of Illinois in 1957 and we have been friends now for over 50 years. When Don graduated from the university he began his career with Libby, McNeil & Libby, the food company in Chicago, later acquired by Nestlé, and worked for that company for his entire career. Don's life and mine were incredibly parallel. We both started our careers in Chicago, both moved to other cities, both married nurses, both had three children, and both have four grandchildren.

Gloria and Don Treash.

Don headed the Human Resources function for Libby and Nestlé and was greatly respected. One of the officers of the company paid him the supreme compliment by telling him, "Don, you understand corporate politics but are not political." The perfect HR man. Since Don and I were so compatible and our wives got along well and our children all played together, we had many great family vacations together. I remember one at Crystal Lake, Michigan, where it rained all week and the mothers had to endure the kids being trapped in the cottage. I remember another vacation to Acadia National Park in Maine where the kids put on a play for us and we went to the peak of Cadillac Mountain early in the morning to be the first people in the United States to see the sun come up that day.

We became members of the Sunrise from Mount Cadillac Club on August, 24, 1978. Don and I have had great discussions over the years about our careers and families. I greatly respect his advice and counsel.

Family Life
CHAPTER IV

Retirement in Minnesota
.... as I Remember it

For the Lord gives wisdom; From His mouth
come knowledge and understanding. He stores
up sound wisdom for the upright; He is a shield
to those who walk in integrity,
— Proverbs 2:6 & 7

In 2001, after 35 years in Rockford, we decided it was time to move on to be closer to our children in Minneapolis. The quality of life in the Twin Cities was also an attraction. Rockford had become a marginal place to live. The school system was a disaster, and it was experiencing an increasingly poor economy. Off the top of my head I was able to list over twenty critical mistakes the city had made during the time we lived there. That explained how it would be rated as one of the ten worst cities in America. Besides, there was not even a church that I had any interest in attending. Despite all these negatives it was a difficult decision for Lura and me because we had a host of great friends there and we were comfortably settled in our home that was paid for.

After I sold my business to Fred Raffety there was no reason why we could not move. I have given advice to many clients that, "You should move before you have to move, otherwise you cannot adjust to a move later in life," and now it was time to act on my own advice. We both agreed to the move, but Lura had the most reservations.

THE PROMISED LAND

We made several trips to Minnesota to search for a new home. Because we could not find a house that we really liked and that met our criteria, we decided to have a home built for us. We signed the papers and gave them a down payment in November, 2001 for the construction of our new home in Eden Prairie (rated one of the top ten cities in the U.S.) to be ready in April. 2002. It met most of our specifications, but not all.

We had planned on downsizing but the new home had 3,800 square feet. The larger home has allowed us to live comfortably, each having our own office and TV, to adequately accommodate many house guests, like a hotel with many amenities, and to host the small group we would soon be leading. We had Paul, Dawn and Carla checking the building site for us and in March there was just the foundation hole, so we knew that April delivery was impossible. We called the builder and he gave us nothing but excuses and indicated that it would be available in September, at the earliest. We were dumbfounded but both individually had the feeling that God did not want us to move yet. It would be a defining moment in our lives.

$\sim$

HEALTH CHALLENGE

In June I went to the eye doctor for a routine examination. After examining my eyes the doctor detected something was wrong and immediately called a specialist. It was the specialist's day off, but he arranged to see me that same day. I had a torn retina. After an hour of painful laser and cryogenic surgery, I got up from the chair but did not feel good.

When Lura arrived to pick me up the doctor called her aside and said I was not reacting normally to the surgery and he recommend I go to the hospital and have a cardio-vascular evaluation. Then he asked me if I could stand up. I said, "no", rather than, "not yet". This created panic and an ambulance was called. At the hospital I received a full cardio workup and was found to have serious build-up of plaque in the arteries leading to my heart that would require a coronary bypass.

After surgery the doctor told Lura that the fifth by-pass he made had me responding better. Because my condition was discovered early enough I did have a heart attack. That was significant thing because it meant I would have no heart damage prior to the surgery. If we had moved in April or May as originally planned I would surely had a heart attack because of all the stress and hard work of the move. The intervention of God was evident. The surgery lasted for four hours and it took me a year to fully recover.

A month after surgery I went to my office and sat with Fred and a client. Fred was greatly concerned because I hardly engaged in any conversation – it was because I was still recovering. The experience impacted me enough to enter therapy and that would be the beginning of a new life style. It changed what we ate and I began working out at the Life Time Fitness Health Club three times a week with a vigorous cardio exercise routine. It changed my whole perspective on life. No longer would I take my health for granted. I began to listen to my body, measure and record my vital signs each week and see my doctor twice a year. The only residual problem was my writing, which gets progressively smaller as I write a sentence. Thankfully, the computer takes care of that problem.

OUR PLANS

As is my custom, I wrote objectives for our new life in Minnesota: finding a home we could live in for at least five years, finding a church that met our needs for spiritual growth and fellowship and where we could serve. Lura hoped to work with a crisis pregnancy center and do post-abortion-syndrome counseling. I wanted to locate a Christian counseling service and serve as a Para-therapist.

The home we selected has provided us with a great quality of life. The condo association provides all of the outside maintenance and the inside cleaning is done by a maid service. This has freed both of us to enjoy our family and the many things available in the Twin Cities. Our home is conveniently located in the middle of a circle with Dawn's home, Carla's home, Wooddale Church and a shopping center all within seven miles. We furnished and decorated our home to be a functional, interesting, inviting and warm place where people would feel at home, rather than trying to create a show piece. It is located next to a bubbling creek in a beautiful setting.

We moved into in our new home on November 1, 2002, and settled in to find a church that both Lura and I felt met our individual needs and met the criteria of our plan.

After visiting several churches, we selected Wooddale, despite the fact it was a mega-church with 10,000 attendees, and we had always preferred smaller ones. We knew Frank and Ginny Doten from Cumberland Church who welcomed us and coached us on what group to join. It was also the church where Carla attended, so that was a plus. The church offers seven services each weekend so there are lots of choices of time and style. Unlike most seniors, we prefer the late contemporary service. We attend a Sunday morning Big Group At Church, called "Second Half" (referring to the second half of life), that has interesting programs and has expanded our world of friends and acquaintances.

Our Wooddale Church Small Group at Home.

We joined a Small Group At Home but soon decided we would like to lead a group of our own. Since we were new to the church and did not know many people, the pastor in charge of Small Groups assigned people to our group. We have a "relationship- type" group of fourteen with five married couples and four singles, an equal number of men and woman, and ages from forties to nineties.

As leaders, it is encouraging to see the spiritual growth of each person as they respond to our leadership and the frequent acts of kindness. Since the inception the members have experienced both insurmountable joy and deep grief, so we have tightly bonded as we share life together. It is the best experience we have had in a Small Group. God led us to the right church where we could minister and be ministered to.

Lura also was looking for a way to use her skills to counsel women in need of help. Significant among those are women in conditions of guilt and depression after undergoing abortions.

Abortion is a blight on our country because it does not respect human life, which is the very core of the nation's soul. Once it is acceptable to take an innocent life, all life is degraded. Disregard for life fosters violent behavior because life has lost its value. All the arguments for abortion (every child a wanted child, a woman should be able to control her own body, it's a glob of tissue not a baby) fall apart when tested with critical thinking and facts. Abortion is contrary to a woman's basic nature - conception, pregnancy, birth, and nurturing - and therefore causes guilt and anger against those who performed it or assisted. After an abortion, for many women the guilt can still be present after ten or twenty years and causes depression and anger that affect their daily lives and their marriages.

Lura was skilled at helping a number of women understand what is going on in their minds and how God's love and forgiveness can heal them. Despite the urgent need for counselors, when she went to the Women's Care Center in Minneapolis to volunteer, they turned her away because she had not had an abortion. The plan did not work but God had other plans for her.

Mary Becker, who we came to know through our large group at church, asked Lura to teach English with an organization called Connexions International to international students at the University of Minnesota. Lura was trained and skilled at teaching English through her experience with Laotians in Rockford. For three years she would faithfully drive the fifteen miles through traffic to the University campus to teach eager students. The purpose of the program is to build international relationships and that is what happened. While we were able to make friends with a number of students, one student and her husband became like family. After two years of conversing about what it means to be a Christian, she accepted Christ. We have come to love them dearly. While teaching English was not in the original plan, God led Lura into meaningful ministry.

After our daughter Carla adopted a child in 2008, Lura

retired from teaching to babysit for her new granddaughter. When Carla adopted Brynn she needed grandmother to baby-sit two days a week, so Lura resigned from teaching. While it is challenging to care for a young child, Lura loves Brynn and enjoys seeing her develop week by week. Carla is a special person who loves children so much that she adopted a child as a single mom. This is a new experience for us, too.

～

When we moved to Minnesota I studied family and marriage counseling, but was never able to locate a suitable organization to work with. One day Bob Strauhn, an attorney and member of the Stadium Village Church, asked me out to lunch. The church wanted to establish Connexions International as a separate entity and he invited me to become a board member.

Having served on many boards over the years I thought it was a situation where I had something to offer. After four years as an active board member and Treasurer, we have developed a program serving almost one thousand international students a year with a director and about thirty volunteers. We use the free English lessons as a bridge to build relationships whereby students can be introduced to Christianity. This approach has been fruitful and I believe I have made a contribution to the kingdom even though it was not part of my original plan.

～

About the time we moved to Eden Prairie, Paul Sjolund's brother, Dave, wanted to go into business. He asked me to assist him in finding, evaluating and purchasing a business. After a number of attempts, we located a business in Columbia, South Carolina, that was a perfect fit for him. He named the company Accutech Machining and I became a director. This was not part of the original

The Alexander Family Reunion in 2005.

plan but has provided an outlet for applying my many
years of business experience.

Another thing Lura and I were able to do because we
had moved to Minnesota was to co-sponsor an Alexander
Family Reunion with Paul and Dawn in the Twin-Cities.
The Alexanders had a long tradition of having a family
reunion every three or four years. Plans need to be made
two years in advance because we need to co ordinate with
all the family members who live outside the U.S. – Hong
Kong, Japan, Ukraine, Taiwan, and Indonesia. These
events are high priority with all the family members, even
those who are family members by marriage. Everyone had
a great time hanging around with each other and enjoying
all the things offered in Minneapolis

∽

50 YEARS TOGETHER

2008 was our 50th wedding anniversary and the
original plan was to celebrate with an informal picnic at
the Minnesota Landscape Arboretum inviting family and
just a few very close friends. However, it quickly turned

into a formal dinner party complete with a wedding cake with 35 people attending including the extended family, neighbors and many friends. We invited people who had made us feel welcome to Minnesota. We all had a wonderful time. It was held in June rather than September, our actual date, so Bill and Yasuko could attend. Bill acted as mêlée. (In October we went on a second honeymoon trip to Disneyland in Orlando, Florida.)

At the anniversary dinner I gave some remarks about the meaning of marriage and ended with a love poem to honor Lura.

When you were young and twenty one, a name, Lura, unknown to me,
How could I know that you would be the one alone to set me free?

Twas Adam, first of man, who cried, "Thank God, this Eve, for me he planned."
Like him, I too with joy surprised, met you because God so designed.

All others then were lost and gone; at last my heart to them had died.
That place was filled by you alone, secure, complete, satisfied.

And now that you are seventy-one, unchanged you really are to me;
The luster of your former self is outlined in you still.

I loved you then, I love you now
I'm sure, Lura, I always will

– Adopted from a poem by Ken Jacobs,
Roseville, Minnesota

When we told people we were retiring to Minnesota they thought we were crazy moving north, but it has turned out just fine. While the winters are long and harsh, the rest of the year is wonderful and more than make up for the winter. We do, however, look forward to global warming!

We have become Minnesotans, learning how to deal with the cold winters with warm clothing, a remote starter for the car and a cozy fireplace so it does not interfere with our lifestyle of church, concerts, family times, health club visits, shopping, etc. In hindsight it was the right move because we get to spend time with our family. God gave us the wisdom to make the right decision.

Adventures
CHAPTER V

Foreign Travel .... as I Remember it

*The rich and the poor have a common
bond The Lord is the maker of them all.*
                    — Proverbs 22:2

There are few things that change your perspective on
life more than travel outside the United States.

We have traveled in more than 30 countries; the rich
nations of the world such as - Japan, Germany, Austria
and Switzerland and the poor countries of the world like -
Guatemala, Mozambique and the Philippines. Each
country has its own culture and its own landscape. One
sees the difference the culture makes, but the same basic
humanity shows in people in every country. Some are
happy and content; others are stoic, sad or hopelessly
downtrodden.

When we plan a trip we do not just think about
adventure and enjoyment. We plan trips with a purpose to
learn about the culture or the history and to build relationships that bond and/or to encourage people, especially
missionaries.

$\sim$

HONG KONG

In 1979 we took our first family trip to a foreign
country to visit Harry and Lyn (Lura's sister) Ambacher
in Hong Kong. Hong Kong became a British Colony in
1842, with a few remote fishing villages, and was ceded
back to China in 1997. Today it has a population of 7
million, many who are escapees from main land China,

and is one of most densely populated cities in the world. At that time Ambachers lived on Yuet Wah Street in a densely populated area of Kowloon where buildings are built side by side leaving no open space for trees or grass.

The crowded street was lined with shops and street vendors, all of whom welcome your business. One shop offered fish cut in half with hearts still beating to show freshness.

There we saw how missionaries lived and worked. I volunteered to fix their poorly functioning toilet. When I tried to turn off the water, the valve handle crumbled in my hand because of the corrosion from the

A crowded market in Hong Kong.

ocean salt water used to conserve fresh water. When I went to the store for replacement parts, I found there was no standard plumbing in Hong Kong, so every toilet is different. No parts were available, so I had to improvise.

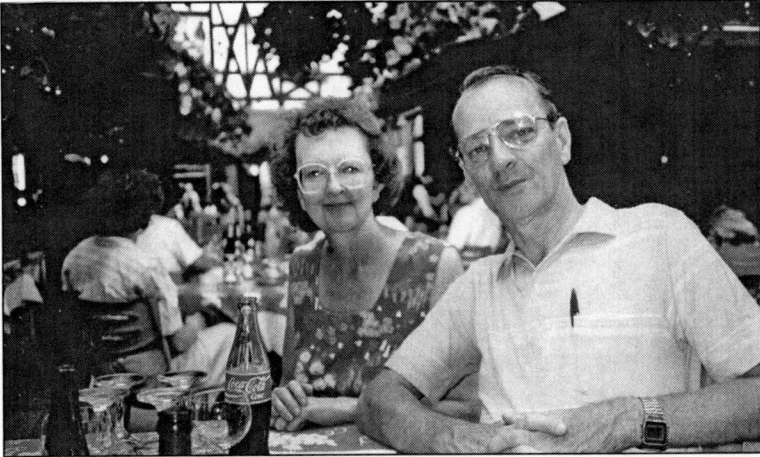

The Ambachers, Lura's sister Lyn and her husband Harry, both workers in the development of churches. It is remarkable how God has blessed the work of Christians who have demonstrated how to build an indigenous church that is not dependent on missionaries.

I learned how time consuming it is to just do the routine tasks of daily living. I would estimate when living in another culture it takes an additional two hours per day (fourteen hours per week for two people) for additional shopping, travel time and for meal preparation and clean up. There were no microwaves or dishwashers and additional trips to the store were necessary because you have to hand-carry your groceries.

Their traffic congestion was the worst in the world. Of course this puts stress on time for ministry. Don't think that a missionary hiring a local maid/nanny is a luxury. It is more like a relief from the time-consuming chores of daily living so there is more time for family and ministry. Unlike most of the missionaries in Hong Kong who lived in the better areas, the Ambachers sacrificed by choosing to live close to their workplace to save travel time and to be able to entertain students in their home.

When we arrived we went to a restaurant in an outlying area and had our first experience with chop sticks. There was no silverware available, so I left still feeling hungry. This was the first of many new experiences we would have, like seeing people actually worshipping idols, using joss sticks for fortune telling, burning paper objects to send to their deceased family, and visiting eerie Buddhist Temples where you could feel the powers of evil. At the temples there were persistent beggars, so Lyn taught me my first Cantonese word which sounded like a cat. When I used the MEOW sound to ward them off, they just continued, but then I remembered it was MEU, like a kitten, which worked.

Because Christianity is a western religion, even in Hong Kong the traditional hymns are a part of worship, but the words are in Cantonese. Lura, asked to play the piano, lost her place and could not find it because the people were singing in Cantonese.

Carla was with us and wanted to buy a gift for her friend Christine so we went shopping. After visiting several stores she found just the right gift at a store with a counter that was barely six feet wide. I asked the price and it seemed reasonable, so I said we would buy it. The store clerk looked confused and went off to confer with the store owner. When she returned she said, "I will give you a new customer discount." I had neglected to bargain, so she did not know how to handle the transaction with such a naive buyer.

The Ambacher's were church planters using the method of "Study Centers" for building relationships with students in 13- story high-rise apartment buildings. They started from scratch and after thirty years of labor had planted twenty-eight churches and started a seminary-Bible school which graduates Chinese leaders for serving the churches. It is remarkable how God blessed their work of demonstrating how to build an indigenous church not dependent on missionaries. I deeply respect Harry and Lyn for their effort, vision and dedication.

After returning home, Pastor Hanstad at our home church asked me to give a report on our visit to Hong Kong following the Sunday evening church service. As I was sitting waiting to be introduced, I was overcome with a feeling of doom. All the energy in my body seemed to dissipate, and I felt the presence of evil. I prayed and the presence left and I was able to report on God's work in Hong Kong but it was clear to me that Satan did not want the facts known.

∽

NEW ZEALAND

After I retired from Focus Financial Advisors, we went on a month long trip to New Zealand with Don and Gloria Treash and Keith and Diane Lindley. We rented a van at the Auckland airport and Keith took over the driving because he knew how to drive on the left hand side of the road. However, within a few miles he ran over a curb in the street and blew a tire. The van was all new to us, so we could not find the car jack and had to call for help. That is how the adventure began.

We spent 2 days touring around in Auckland, where we visited Kelly Tarlton's famous Antarctica underwater exhibit located on a beautiful bay with sail boats keeled over by a strong wind puffing out their sails. Then we started traveling south on the North island visiting the Tongariro National Park with it's Taranaki Falls, the Maori Arts and Crafts Center with Maori Indians entertaining us, and the city of Rotorua with its bubbling thermo fields and therapeutic hot springs pools of water at different temperatures, which we tried out. We also visited a family that Don and Gloria knew from Connecticut. They were grateful to see friends from the States and they told us a lot about the country of New Zealand.

At the very south tip of the north island is the beautiful

capital city of Wellington. There we met an interesting couple who operated a lovely bed and breakfast which included a sumptuous breakfast. They told us how they had found a personal relationship with Christ later in life but were remorseful because their two adult sons were not believers. Wellington reminds me of Seattle because it is located by the ocean on a hill and has beautiful gardens. It is one of the few cities outside the United States where I think I would enjoy living (Cape Town, South Africa, Vienna, and Salzburg, Austria being the others.)

After a two and one half hour ferry ride across Cook Strait to the south island, we visited the Abel Tasman National Park and the City of Nelson, named after the English naval hero Horatio Nelson. I found Nelson a fascinating city because it had solved the problem, common to many older U.S.

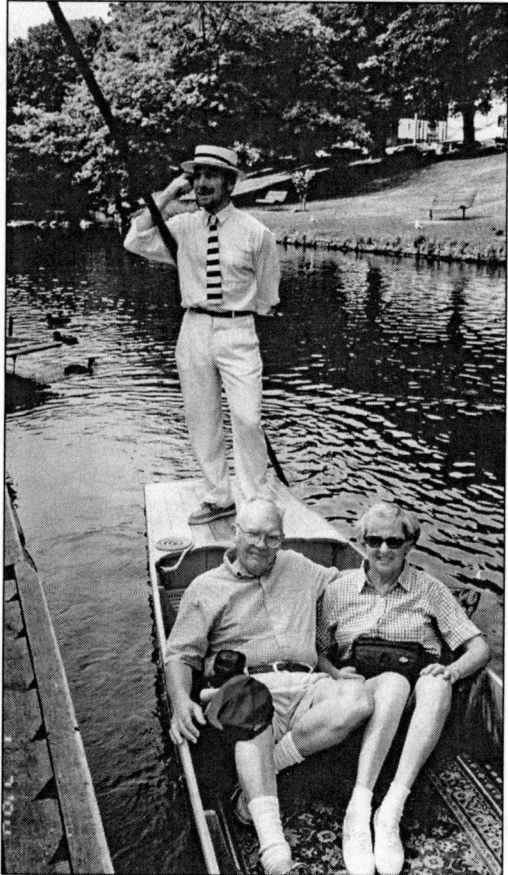

At Christchurch, Lura and I went punting down the Avon in a boat propelled and guided by an attendant with a long pole.

cities, including Rockford, of creating a viable downtown with ample parking. They accomplished this by demolishing buildings in a core and replacing them with making parking lots, and leaving the existing store buildings around the perimeter. From there we went to the city of Christchurch where we toured beautiful botanical gardens and went punting down the Avon River in a flat bottom boat propelled by a long pole while romantic music played in the background.

Black-water-rafting was next. Yes, black not white, because you travel down an underground river in a cave. It turned out to be one of the most adventurous things we have ever done. We arrived at a small store in the middle of nowhere where we boarded a van and were taken to a shed where we changed into wet suits, rubber boots and a miner's hard hat, complete with a light. Next the van took us to an open field where there was a small hole in

Down and under in New Zealand. here we are shown with full gear, about to enter a hole in the ground and down a ladder 25 feet into a cave and to a hidden river.

the ground. We slipped through the hole, which was almost too small for Don, and climbed down a steel ladder about 25 feet into a cave. Because it had not rained recently, the water level in the cave was low so we had to climb over slick rocks and boulders for a mile. The cave temperature was cooler than my body so it made my glasses steam up and I could not see where I was going. I had to feel my way along the tunnel. We finally reached deeper water, climbed on to our large inner-tubes, and floated down the stream for a mile or two. The cooler water temperature refreshed us after over heating in the rubber suits.

We stopped to rest and our guide instructed us to turn off all of our lights. Caves have total darkness but we could see because of the light of glow-worms on the ceiling. We finally saw daylight and squeezed out of the cave totally exhausted. We asked the guide if he had ever had customers our age before and he said, "No." We understood why!

∽

We proceeded on, passing through Arthur's National Park with some of the most beautiful mountain ranges in the world, to Franz Josef where we flew in a helicopter for a breathtaking ride up to the top of a glacier. Glacier Valley was quite a thrill.

Milford Sound on the southwest corner of the south island was our next stop. We were in for an adventure of a lifetime. We did a three day trek though the rainforest. We were grateful that it did not rain while we were there. It was an exhausting 10.2 mile hike because the roots and rocks on the path required constant vigilance with every step. We spent the first night at well-furnished Pyke Lodge, located deep in the forest, with great food for our starved bodies, hot showers, and comfortable beds. We finally reached Martin's Bay Lodge, where we fished and saw sea lions resting on the rocks and beaches.

From Franz Josef, a helicopter took us to the top of a glacier.

At Milford Sound at the southwest corner of South Island, Lura and I did a three-day 10.2 mile trek through the rainforest. They were grateful that it did not rain.

At the end of the third day we were flown out by a
small plane. It was a great experience.

Next it was on to Queenstown which we used as a base
point to go down to InverCargill on the south shore of the
south island where we visited with Pastor Barry and
Claire Ayers. We had first met them at a training seminar
at the Willow Creek Church in Barrington, Illinois, and
promised to visit them when we went to New Zealand.
It was out of our way, but it turned out be a highlight of
our trip, visiting their church and having an authentic
New Zealand dinner in their home. Our visit was fun and
a great encouragement to them which they needed at that
time. After church they asked if we would like to see the
car collection of one of their members Bill and Shona
Richardson. I expected to see two or three cars, but was
overwhelmed by what we saw - two large buildings full of
antique cars, trucks and even a gas tanker. Here at the end
of the earth was a world renowned car collection.

New Zealand is one of our favorite places. The people
were genuinely friendly, they speak English, have western
food, and a beautiful country. Their only problem is that
New Zealanders drive on the wrong (left) side of the road
because of their English heritage. We would like to return,
but New Zealand is a long, long way to go.

∽

GUATEMALA

We arrived at the Guatemala City airport and Keith
and Diane Lindley were there to meet us. Don and Gloria
Treash would join us shortly and we would have another
great adventure. Gloria knew Diane from nurse's training.
Diane met Keith on a mission trip to Guatemala, they
married, and both were serving as missionaries with
Missionary Ventures. This mission organization provides
opportunities for church groups coming on short-term

mission projects.

Unlike New Zealand, there was no time change for us, so without jet lag we immediately began to see the capitol city of Guatemala, with its historic government square, National Palace, Catholic Church, and armed guards everywhere. While New Zealand is a wealthy country, Guatemala is one of the poorest countries in the world with a Gross National Income per person per year of just $2,400.

We went to a slum area, to the Victorino Mesquital Feeding Center, and gave a Bible lesson to some children. I had never seen such poverty; one home was built with cardboard boxes on the side of a hill. One single water spigot served hundreds of families and most homes were crammed in side by side and constructed of corrugated steel panels, used lumber, or mud bricks. I told a Bible story to the children. We visited a feeding center near some railroad tracks. People who live there are squatters using the railroad right-of-way to build themselves a shack. The children are served lunch, their only nutritious meal of the day, and are told about Jesus' love for them. We still give regularly to support this wonderful ministry.

∽

While eastern Guatemala is jungle, the western part is semi-arid plateau and mountains. We traveled by Jeep across the west and then northwest into the mountains near the Mexican border. We saw Zacaleu Ruins (Mayan pyramids), and a number of schools and churches. Don and I had the opportunity to speak at one of the churches.

All the roads were rough but the mountain roads were rough and dangerous. Fortunately, Keith knew the restaurants we could safely visit along the way so we did not get sick. He drove at night up the mountain roads through rain, fog and clouds to the remote village of Nebaj where we spent the night in the Hospedaje El Rinconsito Hotel.

Overnight in Rabaj

Lura and I spent a night at the Hosedaje El Rinconsito Hotel.

In the morning there were a pig and a chicken in the courtyard.

The rooms were primitive at best, bare except for beds with 2x4 frames and a plywood base covered by a thin blanket.

Keith picked it because it had hot water.

That night we were assigned our rooms which turned out to be primitive at best bare except for beds with a 2 X 4 frame and a plywood base covered with a thin blanket. We could hardly sleep on such a hard surface and woke up the next morning stiff and hurting. Our room was the only one with electricity, so we had to share. In the morning I dropped my toothbrush into the horse trough, which was the only place to wash up, and had to bottom fish to retrieve it. The toilet was so foul the women would not use it and waited for hours until they found a suitable place. We did not use the hot showers because of the icky conditions. In the morning there was a pig and a chicken in the courtyard, so we planned on bacon and eggs for breakfast, but instead had black beans.

Up in the mountains we visited an orphanage where children were rescued from poor families. Families are so poor that they cannot afford black beans, a staple in the Guatemalan diet. They had only ground corn to eat and so were willing to give up their children so they would not starve. Now that is real poverty. After roughing it, we went to Atitlan, near Guatemala's largest lake, and had a nice hotel. It is a beautiful area and we shopped there for bargains. We returned to Guatemala City to fly home. We had seen a beautiful country with lots of wonderful people, encouraging believers and experiencing missions in action. It is a trip we will always remember.

ᑫᑐ

MOZAMBIQUE AND SOUTH AFRICA

Wooddale Church has a significant ministry in Mozambique, investing $100,000 per year, part of it being economic development. Lura and I, Pastor Leith Anderson and his wife Charleen and six others from Wooddale went to evaluate the progress being made through Micro Loans.

Mozambique is located on the southeast corner of Africa on the Indian Ocean. The history of the country is tragic. It was victim to the slave trade for 100 years, with a million people taken. There were 475 years under Portuguese colonial rule (1498-1975) when natural resources were extracted and little was done to develop production capability that would improve the life of the Mozambique people. The country was under a socialist Communist domination for 8 years (1975-1983) and then a dreadful 17 years of civil war (1975-1992) with 5.7 million people displaced out a total population of 20 million. Finally in 1994 peace was achieved, with a multi-party democracy and free market system. But then

HIV/AIDS came, affecting 16 percent of the population with 60,000 deaths per year, destroying the family and leaving thousands of orphans.

Since 1994 the country has had democratic elections and a free economy, but lack of human resources has perpetuated severe poverty. The Gross National Income per capita per year is $1,215. When the Portuguese left the country they destroyed everything of value. Less than 1,000 people in the whole country had the equivalent of a high school educa-tion. Currently the country suffers from a "brain drain". As soon as people are educated they leave the country for better opportunities else-where. The country has great natural resources, so the challenge is to make the country as wealthy out of the ground as it is under the ground. This

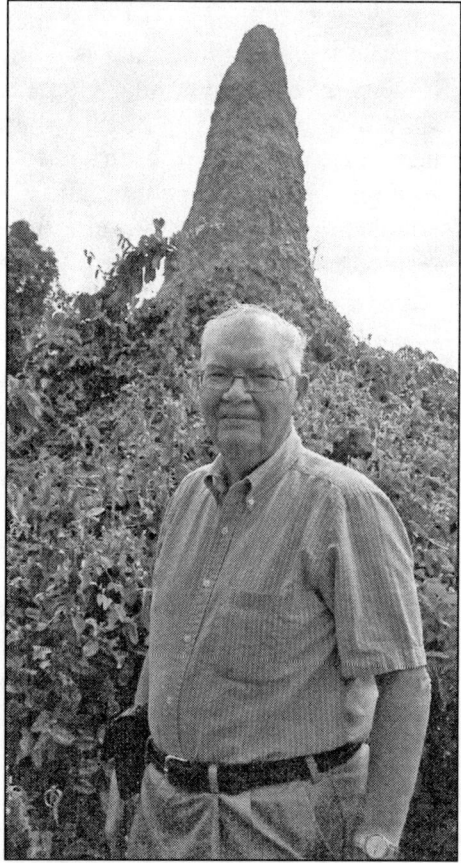

Behind me – a giant ant hill.

means education, health services, Christian values, and empowering people with business knowledge and access to capital.

Our adventure started with a 10,000 mile flight to Amsterdam and then on to a flight over the snow-capped

French Alps, the gleaming Mediterranean Sea, the brown sands of the great Sahara Desert, the green of equatorial Africa, green so dark it looked black, landing in Johannesburg, South Africa and then flying to Maputo, Mozambique. That is a long way!

After getting settled in our hotel we began a hectic schedule of visiting places all over the country operated by World Relief and its companion organization Africa Works. We traveled hundreds of miles by van over washboard roads (they do not have graders) and by air around the country.

We visited an egg incubation facility (one of the community's small chicken ranches where chicks are grown into marketable birds), irrigation projects, mango and papaya groves, and a coconut processing project, a cashew factory, a refugee camp, and a farm growing plants that produce seeds used as a diesel-fuel additive. We even saw giant ant hills that are as hard as concrete

The refugee camps of Nampula are not what you see on TV –not a place of the hopeless and hungry eyes

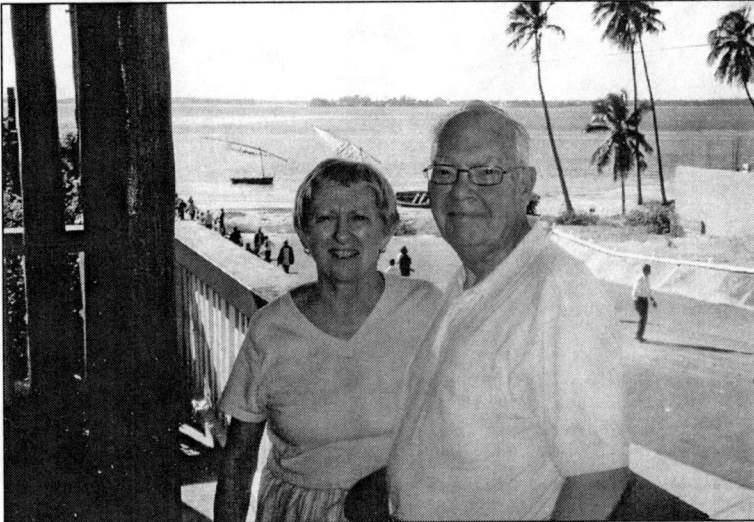

A break at a beachside resort on the Indian Ocean.

We had a wonderful time with the children.

behind a barbed wire fence. It is an open community of happy people working to support themselves. We saw a training facility for teaching metal- working, carpentry, sewing, and computer skills. They had built a dike and had water for irrigating crops, egg laying hens to provide protein for their diet and chicks being raised to provide cash income. They had a health clinic and several churches. Everything was clean and orderly. It was a real credit to the Mozambique government and World Relief.

Because Leith Anderson was a World Relief board member and we were joined by the organization's President, Sammy Mah, and his wife, we received VIP treatment. We were invited to meet with the U.S. Ambassador to Mozambique and his staff at the embassy where they told us about the millions of dollars and AIDS medications being poured into the country. Later the Ambassador invited us to a cocktail party at his personal residence. One Mozambique AIDS worker asked me to thank President George W. Bush for medications which are the difference between life and death. President Bush may be responsible for saving more lives than any person in history.

We met with the Mozambique Minister of Commerce who proudly told us about the "One Stop Shopping"

Lura outside a hut in a remote village where the visiting women stayed the one night they were there. The men were housed separately.

program to speed up the permits to operate a business in
Mozambique. I stressed the need for training to make
the country more productive and competitive in world
markets, but realistically there is little incentive to be
more productive when labor is so cheap and capital is so
expensive and unemployment is 70%. We had to walk up
six flights of stairs to his office because the elevators
were not working, which proved my point!

One night we attended an appreciation dinner, hosted
by World Relief, for all the influential church pastors in
the Maputo area. At our table we were seated with three
pastors and their wives and got real insight into their
ministries. The buffet was the most splendid array of food
I have ever seen. The evening was a real tribute to these
key pastors and their wives.

During our travel throughout the country we stayed at
first class hotels except for two nights. One hotel was like
the one we stayed at in Guatemala, except the beds were
lumpy rather than hard, and the second night was in a
native hut in a remote village where we slept barracks-
style. It was an interesting experience because we could
see how people lived in primitive conditions without the
trappings of the outside world. They reported seventeen
women had been lost to crocodiles while washing clothes
in the river.

We learned about the Africa Works program and why
it is successful. The key to success is that you do not give
them anything except business training and loans. Giving
promotes a mentality of, "If I stay poor, people keep
giving more." After selecting those who exhibit entrepreneurial spirit, they are provided with counsel on how to
operate a business and how to handle money, pay back
the loan, invest part for the future and live on the rest.
All this is counter-cultural to them, but the loan payback
is 98%, so the program is successful. They earn about an
extra $80 per month.

Our group was so impressed with the African leadership – Sam Gratus and Sammy Gumba and many others –

and the success of the program. Although our gift was modest, our group gave a total of over $800,000 to the loan program.

∾

After our visit to Mozambique, Lura and I flew down to Cape Town, South Africa, for a few days of vacation. Cape Town is one of the most beautiful cities in the world, spread out between the deep blue of the Atlantic Ocean and with the magnificent Table Mountain serving as a backdrop for the city.   We saw the city with its historic castle, a busy ocean waterfront, Robben Island prison where Nelson Mandela was imprisoned for 27 years under apartheid (Lura tried out his cell) and then went on to become President. A ride down the coast to the Cape of

Cape Town, on the beautiful and interesting Cape of Good Hope where the Indian Ocean meets the Atlantic. In South Africa, we stopped there and in Johannesburg on our trip to Mozambique.

**Lura stood in a prison cell on Robben Island
where black civil rights leader Nelson Mandela was
imprisoned for 27 years during the time of the racial
segregation policy Apartheid. The policy was overcome
after a long struggle, and Mandela went on to become
president of South Africa.**

Good Hope was breathtakingly beautiful and interesting.
One of the interesting things is the penguins nesting on
the windblown beaches. There are seven species but only
three live in Antarctica.

   Like New Zealand, South Africa is close to the South
Pole that there are Penguins. You could see where the
light blue of the Indian Ocean meets the dark blue of the
Atlantic. It was a great adventure we will never forget
because we saw God's people working for His kingdom
under difficult conditions.

POVERTY

Poverty is a dreadful thing. Of the world's people, 20% live on less than $1.25 per day and 48% live on less than $2.50. Nearly 1 billion people are unable to read or sign their name. 1.1 billion people do not have access to clean water and 2.6 billion lack basic sanitation. In most countries someone needs to be paid-off to get permission to start a business or to not enforce a law. We live in a world where you cannot support yourself with just two hands; you need some kind of skill or capital to make it. That is why international trade and micro-loans are so important in the long- term eradication of poverty and why Lura and I gave our largest single gift to provide loans to the poor people of Mozambique.

∽

A MOST-MOVING EXPERIENCE

What are the things that make the U.S. different from the rest of the world? Our freedom, individualism, innovation, capitalist free enterprise system and Christian-based culture with its work ethic and honesty are the things that create wealth. There is no other country that can make things happen like the Americans.

When you get off a plane after spending time in another country you can feel the freedom.

One of the most moving experiences of my life was on a return flight from Athens, Greece, when the passengers spontaneously began singing America The Beautiful.

> *O beautiful for spacious skies,*
> *For amber waves of grain,*
> *For purple mountain majesties*
> *Above the fruited plain!*
> *America! America!*

God shed his grace on thee
And crown thy good with brotherhood
From sea to shining sea

O beautiful for patriot dream
That sees beyond the years
Thine alabaster cities gleam
Undimmed by human tears!
America! America!
God shed his grace on thee
Till nobler men keep once again
Thy whiter jubilee!

It was an emotional experience and it brought tears to my eyes.

Where we have traveled

YEAR	COUNTRY	PLACES VISITED
1955	KOREA	Inchon, Seoul, Pusan, Taegu, Kojin. *See Military Years, Chapter VI.*
	JAPAN	Tokyo & Yokohama. R & R from Korea. Saw the Ginza, Imperial Place, bought a tea set for my mother and had a visit with a missionary.
1972	MEXICO	Mexico City. Played detective. *See Business Years, Chapter VII.*
	CANADA	Lac des Mille Lake, Ontario
1973	CANADA	Lake Louise, Banff.
1974	CANADA	Lac des Mille Lake.
1975		Camping/fishing trips with son Bill
1979	HONG KONG	Kowloon & Victoria Island One of the world's busiest seaports and densely populated places. Visit with the Ambachers. *See Foreign Travel, Chapter V.*
1980	MEXICO	Mexico City. Business trip with Lura. Saw the Aztec Pyramids.
1986	JAPAN	Tokyo.
1989	GERMANY	Frankfurt, Rudesheim, Koblenz, Worms, Baden Baden, Heidelberg Boat ride down the Rhine River
	SWITZERLAND	Zurich, Berne, Interlaken, Grindewald, Ballenberg (Berne means bear, seen there in a zoo.)
	AUSTRIA	Up to the top of Jungfraujoch Mountain, Innsbrook, Salzburg Visited the grounds of 1976 Winter Olympics at Innsbrook. Salzburg is one of my favorite cities, birthplace of Mozart. Toured the castle on the mountain and Hitler's Eagle Nest.
	LIECHTENSTEIN	Liechten In a restaurant I ordered ostrich, confusing it with chicken.

Where we have traveled

YEAR	COUNTRY	PLACES VISITED
1990	**JAPAN**	Osaka, Kobe, Kyoto, Hiroshima, Nagoya. Travel with son Bill and the Wardens. Visited the Hiroshima Nuclear Holocaust Museum, visited the Gold & Silver Pavillions, walked the Path of Contemplation, and stayed at the Min Shuku, a small Japanese Inn. Saw Himeji Castle.
1992	**GUATEMALA**	Guatemala City, Atitian, La democracia, Nebaj, Antigua *See Chapter V.*
1994	**CANADA**	Nova Scotia – Cape Breton. Drove the Cabot Trail. Had a fascinating dinner with friends. Visited the Alexander Graham Bell Museum.
1996	**ISRAEL**	Bethlehem, Jerusalem, Tel Aviv, Megiddo. Walked where Jesus walked.
	GREECE	Athens, Corinth, Mikonos, Patmos. Stood where Paul preached on Mars Hill. Attended an opera and walked through the quaint part of the city in the evening.
	TURKEY	Kusadasi (Ephesus). Visited one of the most interesting cities in the World.
1997	**SWITZERLAND**	Zurich, Geneva, Matterhorn, Bern. Hiked the mountains around the Matterhorn.
	FRANCE	Paris
	ENGLAND	London, Greenwich. Visited Tower of London, St.Paul's Cathedral, Big Ben, Naval Museum.
1998	**PHILIPPINES**	Cebu
	HONG KONG	

Where we have traveled

YEAR	COUNTRY	PLACES VISITED
1999	NEW ZEALAND	Auckland, Hamilton, Rotorua, Wellington, Nelson, Christchurch,Milford Sound, Queenstown, Inver Cargill, Franz Josef Glacier.
2000	CANADA	
	U.S. VIRGIN ISLANDS	St.Thomas, St. Johns Snorkeled in the beautiful warm waters.
	BRITISH VIRGIN ISLANDS	Tortola. Sailed by private yacht.
	PUERTO RICO	
	FRANCE	Paris
2003	AUSTRIA	Vienna
	HUNGARY	Budapest
	CZECH REPUBLIC	Prague
	SLOVAKIA	
2004	BURMUDA	Hamilton Ocean swimming, Naval Museum.
2005	ITALY	Rome, Siena, Pisa, Assisi, Florence, Venice
	VATICAN CITY	Vatican
2006	GERMANY	Munich
2007	MOZAMBIQUE	Maputo, Nampula
	SOUTH AFRICA	Johannesburg, Cape Town, Cape of Good Hope
	NETHERLANDS	Amsterdam
2008	GUATEMALA	Guatemala City, Antiqua

Adventure

CHAPTER VI

The Military Years
.... as I Remember them

The fear of the Lord is the beginning of wisdom
— Psalms 1:7

My first thoughts about the Army were to put my mind in neutral and follow the rest of the robots. I thought I could not learn or accomplish anything during my term in the service. It turned out to be worse than I originally thought. I was treated like dumb trash for two years that precluded any noble feelings of pride about serving my country.

Drafted into service and going into a situation of unknowns with no support system, no church, no family, no Christians would test my faith. Could my spiritual battery last two years? Little did I know what God had in store for me. But I did learn a few valuable lessons, accomplish something of lasting significance and grew more confident in my faith.

∽

LESSONS LEARNED

I REMEMBER my first day. I got up very early in the morning and with my parents traveled to downtown Chicago to the induction center where they left me after a short prayer. There I pledged to protect and defend the Constitution of the United States of America and underwent a physical exam. The doctor's head dropped when he listened to my extremely slow heart but he didn't even put a note in my record. I would learn later on that there was no such thing as a personal medical record, at least one that was used. **Lesson No, 1: If you are warm, you're in.**

~

ARMY TRAINING

From the induction center we were marched to the railroad station and loaded onto a train headed to Fort Leonard Wood, Missouri. About 2 a.m. the next day we arrived and were taken to a barracks to learn how to make a bed but did not get to use it. I was immediately assigned to K. P. were I spent the entire day washing pots, pans and dinner trays. After 36 hours without sleep I was deeply depressed with the thought that I had 729 days to go.

After returning to the barracks I found that most of the men in my unit had spent the day relaxing. Thereafter, whenever there was a formation of troops I would get in the third row near the middle. Work groups are almost always selected from the first row or the fourth row or off the ends. **Lesson No. 2: Someone has to do the work, so don't put yourself in a position where you will be picked to do it.**

Since I was inducted just before Christmas, we were assigned to a temporary barracks. When we arrived at the barracks we found it ankle deep in trash. The barracks had been inhabited by about ten black men from South Carolina. We were ordered to clean the barracks, but as soon as The Sergeant was out of sight, the black men starting leaving. One of the guys called out, "Where are you guys going?" The reply was, "If you want it clean, clean it up yourselves." They seemed to be willing to live in filth and be too lazy to even clean it up. Having come from a good home, it never occurred to me that people could live like that. **Lesson No. 3: Some people's cultural values differed from mine.**

I was assigned to the Sixth Armored Division, 6th Quartermaster Battalion, Company B for Basic Training lasted eight long weeks. While out on bivouac, I was passing through another unit's area when a Sergeant stopped me and with his steely eyes ordered me to chop firewood for his pot-bellied stove. Since he had taken my rifle, there was no way for me to escape. So I chopped him a nice pile of wood just long enough not to fit in his stove. Not noticing this, he gave me back my rifle and I ran away like a Cheetah chasing prey. **Lesson No. 4: Never directly confront the system, and always use passive-aggressive means to get even.**

The patch of the 6th Armored Division.

I learned about physical training, and lost almost 20 pounds in the process. Also, I learned how to get along with little sleep, and when I did sleep, to do it under any conditions. I didn't feel a lot stronger but had plenty of endurance to do anything. **Lesson No. 5: Basic training worked. I was invincible!**

After basic training I was assigned to Intermediate Radio Operator's School at Fort Knox, Kentucky. For eight weeks, I learned Morse code and for five days a week it was Dit, Da, Dit, Dit, Da. I passed the course but was never a proficient radio operator because of my mental inability to carry more than five characters. After Radio School I was assigned to Communications Chief School at Fort Benning near Columbus, Georgia. I learned a lot during 12 weeks that I would apply later in Korea. One day I was able to leave the base and go into town. Because there were a number of soldiers, we all sat together in the back of the bus. As we approached town the bus driver did a strange thing. He stopped the bus and asked us to move to the front of the bus. As the bus traveled on, we came to the part of town where black people lived. When they boarded the bus they all took the seats in the back of the bus. One white woman who was seated in the middle of the bus even moved to the front to make more seating available for the blacks. Had we realized what was going on, I think we would have refused to move. **Lesson No. 6: Jim Crow was still alive in 1954.**

After Communications School I was eventually assigned to a Corps level Camouflage Company at Fort Riley, Kansas and was in charge of a Message Center. I "had it made", which is the goal of every soldier, because all it involved was getting and processing mail. While off duty at a church in Manhattan, Kansas, I for the first time saw my future bride Lura. We did not spend any time together because she was a high school girl and I was a soldier, but we had a number of mutual friends. In Kansas, fathers have shotguns! This was the only time in two years in the service where I had a church and Christian friends. One of my friends, Don Rose, was an officer with a K- 9 unit. I took him to church where Pastor John Ironside (son of the well known evangelist Harry) preached a salvation message, and we prayed together as Don went forward to accept Christ.

When I first arrived at Fort Riley I was assigned to an infantry company of the 1st Infantry Division. All the company did was go out on field exercises followed by guard duty and K.P. I was deeply depressed with the prospects of spending the next eighteen months with this

unit. The situation seemed hopeless. However, the next
morning I was called into Command Post (C.P.) and
reassigned. No one had told me the assignment was
temporary just to provide me with a place to eat and sleep.
**Lesson No. 7: Never assume anything is permanent in
the Army, or in life.**

An ancient proverb says, "This too will pass." I was
shortly levied for Korea

◠

KOREA

After an enjoyable leave at home, I reported to
Fort Lewis near Seattle, Washington, to be processed for
transport to Korea via a troop ship. The ship had not even
left Puget Sound when we encountered a severe storm.
I had never seen such misery with 3,000 seasick men all
vomiting at the same time. When we reached Korean
waters, even before land was in sight, the sea turned
orange due to erosion.

South Korea was a desperately poor, devastated
country ravaged by two wars and a cruel occupation by
the Japanese. As with most poor countries, many of the
women were prostitutes and the men unemployed. The
capital city of Seoul was a bombed-out shell of buildings
from the fighting between the Americans and the North
Koreans. The country had no trees because the Koreans
had cut them down during the Japanese occupation in
order to survive. The Koreans were an interesting people.
While normally very polite, they had a very short fuse and
could get very angry. **Lesson No. 8: War is Hell.**

When my ship reached the port at Inchon to disembark
there was a seabed of gray mud that stretched a mile over
to land. That is why General Douglas MacArthur had been
advised not to make his landing there. However, he went

The ship had not even left Puget Sound. I had never seen such misery, with 3,000 seasick men vomiting at the same time.

ahead and was successful by using the high tide, one of the world's highest at 32 feet, to make a surprise invasion which was a turning point in the war. We were transported to land by an LST using a dredged channel.

Once on shore we boarded a rickety train for a 150 mile ride to the southern port of Pusan and then were trucked to a camp of the 24th Infantry Division. On the way to the camp I noticed a ship docked in the harbor with an orange bear on the smoke stack and wondered what that could stand for. I was assigned to an infantry rifle company because that was where the vacancy rate was highest. Not one of us new arrivals had even been through the second eight weeks of basic infantry training. It made no difference because we were assigned as Pusan port guards.

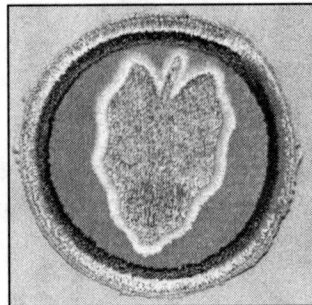

The patch of the 24th Infantry Division.

Sergeant Gritts was our Top Sergeant. He was the scum of the earth and made everyone's life miserable. I hated him with a passion, making him the only man I have ever hated. He took the magazines from the Day Room to his tent before any one else could read them. Being in charge of the mail, I tactfully informed him that they were paid for out of canteen funds and should be left in the Day Room for everyone to read. He chose to take this as a threat to his authority, and I ended up standing before the Company Commander who had little choice but to reprimand me, sentencing me to march around the parade yard with a full back pack for two hours. I considered the punishment an honor because I had confronted the sergeant. My

My field pack.

passive–aggressive strategy kicked in and I filled my pack with blankets and strolled around for a few hours. **Lesson No. 9: Confront evil carefully.**

After being trucked to my assigned guard post, I found out what the orange bear meant - a refrigerator ship! I was assigned to guard the cargo of frozen hams being unloaded by Korean stevedores. When I first arrived I went down into the hold of the ship and found there was no exit except through the hatch, so I observed from the deck. The hold was about zero degrees to keep the hams frozen. Then a Captain came by and ordered me to guard down in the hold of the ship. The fact that I was wearing only light army fatigues was of no concern to him.

As ordered, I went down in the hold but soon began to shiver from the frigid cold and seeing no reason to guard from there, I returned to the deck. Soon the Captain returned and started to reprimand me for not following his direct order.

A sergeant who was standing nearby grasped the situation and said that he had ordered me to the deck. That saved my day, for I would certainly have been court-martialed. I didn't know the Sergeant, where he came from or why he covered for me. He just disappeared. Maybe he was an angel? **Lesson No. 10: There are good people in this world.**

On another occasion I was assigned guard duty to protect a large pile of coal that was stored on the dock. Because so many Koreans had been shot by U.S. soldiers, in some cases over just minor thievery, we were ordered not to shoot anyone stealing less than $25.00. Since there was no way to know the value of what was being stolen, I would not load my rifle but did put on my bayonet because I was walking alone in the dark. When I caught Koreans stealing coal in the middle of the night, I pulled back the bolt on my rifle, which sounded like a round being loaded, and ordered the Koreans to surrender. They shook with fear as I marched them to the Command Post. **Lesson No. 11: Using a passive-aggressive strategy is better than risking a court-martial.**

After a few months of Pusan port guard duty our unit was relocated to the DMZ (Demilitarized Zone) about 25 miles north of the capital city of Seoul in the country's

**On duty at a bunker near the Korean
Demilitarized Zone.**

northwest. In order to understand the DMZ you need to
know how it came about. In 1910, the Japanese invaded
Korea and cruelly occupied the country for 35 years until
the end of World War II, in 1945. At that time the country
was divided at the 38th parallel with the north half given
to the Communists and the south placed in the Free
World. On June 25, 1950, the North Koreans invaded
South Korea and drove the South's unprepared army to
a small perimeter around the southeast city of Pusan.

In September, 1950, while South Korean and American
troops under United Nations authorization precariously
held the Pusan perimeter, General MacArthur made a
surprise attack on the west coast at Inchon and cut off
the main north–south roads and communications routes,
routing the North Korean army. Sensing the opportunity
for total victory, the American-led United Nations army
invaded North Korea and went almost all the way north to
the Yalu River on the China boarder. In December, 1950,

in a surprising counter-attack, the Chinese army attacked and regained control over most of North Korea. The U.N. forces held near the 38th parallel. There was a stalemate until July, 1953, when an agreement was reached to stop the fighting and set up a DMZ. There had been 4 million civilian and military casualties. These included 33,600 American war dead and 92,124 wounded. Our U.N. allies had 16,000 dead and wounded. The military dead and wounded among the other countries in the war included 415,000 South Koreans, 520,000 North Koreans and an estimated 900,000 Chinese. Half of Korea's industry was destroyed and one-third of all homes, and the population was in turmoil. All of this sacrifice was made so the people of South Korea could remain free. Our unit's mission was to enforce the agreement and protect South Korea from invasion or infiltration.

At last, most of the games and making work was over, and I could contribute to something worthwhile. Our base camp was a barbed-wire-fenced compound where a battalion of about 900 men was housed in tents. A battalion consists of four companies with 200 men each plus a Headquarter company with 100 men. The companies would rotate, going up to the DMZ to guard the line and improve our bunkers. From there with binoculars we could see the enemy looking at us through their binoculars. They had three North Korean and two Chinese Divisions opposite our sector, so we were there to just slow them down if they attacked. It was a dangerous place to be, and there were areas not cleared of landmines.

∽

At our base camp there was always a shortage of water. Because the base did not have a source of water it had to be trucked in by a tanker. The tanker trucks had to wait for hours at the central filtration center some miles away so there was no way to know when the truck would arrive back at our base. This was a problem because we never knew when we could refill our five-gallon container. This was the only source of water for the ten men living in our tent to use for washing clothes, bathing, shaving, etc. When there was water, it was very limited, so we had to take a bird-bath in a pan of water. Every six weeks we were trucked to a central bathing facility where we could shower. We really enjoyed a warm shower and the feeling of being clean again.

In order to have our own water supply, the Battalion Commander ordered that a well be dug. They used TNT explosives to blast the hole. The man in charge would shout, "Fire in the hole," followed by a blast and mud flying all over the place. After the well was 30 feet deep and 25 feet wide it gave about one canteen cup of water per hour so the project was abandoned and they hired some Koreans to find a good place to dig a well. With their divining stick they identified a place just a few yards from the original well site. Ten feet down they found all the water we needed. When I wrote home and told my parents about the water shortage, my mother telephoned numerous places trying to find cans of water to send me. Fortunately she never found any.

Life on the DMZ was hard work, building bunkers, sleeping in pup tents, eating cold scrambled eggs in the cold rain and training.

∽

There were lighter moments like when a U.S.O. troop of women from the University of Indiana came to provide some entertainment. Everyone enjoyed their show which had lots of singing and dancing. However, the frontier was no place for women. A building was prepared and used to billet them, but there was only one latrine. Whenever one of the girls had to use the latrine a guard would have to clear the area of men. Then the guard would accompany the women to the latrine. The latrine was built for men and not for modest females. The girls would sit there under the watchful eyes of the guard. Needless to say, the women made as few trips as possible, and there was a long line of men volunteering for guard duty.

❦

As the company Communications Chief, I was responsible for everything electric or electronic. Shortly after we arrived, the Company Commander called me into his office to tell me that our Supply Sergeant had acquired an electric generator and I was to install lights in each tent. Hooking the company generator up to be an alternative power source to the Battalion generator was a challenge, but with my training back at Fort Benning, I figured out how to wire up a three-phase engine.

I did have a few problems. First, I had gone to the motor pool and poured gasoline from a thirty-gallon drum into a five-gallon container to take back to our company area. I poured the gas into the generator, but it would not start no matter how many times I pulled the

Radio-ready.

cord. I eventually discovered that the bung in the top of the thirty-gallon drum was not closed tightly, and rain water had seeped into the drum. Since gas is lighter than water, it was at the top. I did not notice that when I started to pour, the gas came out first, but then the water followed. Once I corrected the problem, the engine started easily. Another problem occurred when I was hooking up the wiring to our generator when the Battalion generator was running. As a safety measure, I stood on a wood board to avoid being grounded and to insulate me from the shock of electricity passing though me into the ground. Then, one of the men standing on the ground inadvertently placed his hand on my shoulder. We both went flying.

Eventually I did get every tent wired with electrical service, so everyone was pleased to have light during the evening hours when the battalion generator was not running. Our company was the only one to have this privilege.

Occasionally I had to go to the Regimental headquarters about one mile from our camp. The roadway was lined with prostitutes who tried very hard to lure me, even grabbing my arm to pull me into their hut. Prostitution was rampant, and one other soldier and I were the only ones in our company who did not frequent them. I did not know him well and do not know if he was a Christian.

As I entered the headquarters building, there was Sergeant Gritts who began to yell and scream at me, as top sergeants are skilled at doing, in front of the entire staff of people because I was so dumb as to wear my hat indoors. He repeatedly did this type of thing to his subordinates, perhaps just to assert his authority, perhaps to hide his inferiority complex. After his tantrum ended I loudly announced that I was "under arms." He then realized that code of conduct requires hats to be removed except when you are carrying a weapon, and I was carrying a rifle. He

left embarrassed and humiliated and without an apology.
Shortly thereafter, he would lose his rank and position as
Top Sergeant because he ordered three Korean women
caught sneaking into our compound to have their heads
shaved. No one cried. **Lesson No. 12: You are smarter
than most people in the Army.**

One day we were called into formation and were told
we would be going on a special mission to guard the
United Nations Neutral Nations Inspection team. As part of
the partitioning agreement each side agreed to inspection.
The South Koreans knew this was a farce and just a means
for the Communists to legally spy on their country. The
South Koreans rioted to protest and the inspectors needed

Our communications jeep.

to be protected. Before we left, our field packs were inspected and a Lieutenant found I had mosquito netting, which he ordered me to leave behind. This would turn out to be a bad decision. On the day we left, we were trucked to an airfield and briefed on our flight. We would be flying over mountainous terrain where there would be no place to land if we had engine trouble, and as a precaution we were issued parachutes. After being instructed on how to count and pull the rip cord we took off and headed for a small emergency landing field on the northeast corner of the country on the Sea of Japan.

Our flight was uneventful, but we landed just clearing some sand dunes, onto a short runway of corrugated metal strips designed for emergency landing for planes shot up over North Korea. We were billeted in a building with open windows and doors. The mosquitoes ate us to death. Because I had no netting I would use a tent tarp as a blanket with just my mouth exposed. In the morning when I woke up my lips would be swollen from mosquito bites. Of course, the Lieutenant was housed in air-conditioned comfort.

∽

While we were there, everyone was assigned to a work crew each morning. For some unknown reason my name was omitted, so I would just disappear, spending the day at the library reading. I still remember two books that I read: Aerial Navigation and Darwin's Origin of the Species. This went on for about two weeks. Meanwhile the South Koreans were causing trouble by broadcasting loud insults and music to the inspectors day and night. Unfortunately it kept us from sleeping too. After a few nights, the Koreans' loud- speaker disappeared, and our commander issued an order for it to be returned. Several weeks later it was found submerged in a barrel of water stored for firefighting. One day, the South Koreans had massed at the front gate and began to riot by using a truck to pull a coil of concertina barbed-wire back from the gate. Our Commander used a bullhorn to warn them that the next attempt would result in shooting. With the next attempt there was a BANG-BANG-BANG and one of the rioters fell, shot in the leg. The riot was over.

One of our work assignments was to remove 12 long poles that were anchored in concrete. The men were ordered to dig night and day in eight hour shifts. After three days of digging only three of the poles had been removed. The men revolted, demanding that a tank-retriever be used to pull the poles up. A tank-retriever came and wrapped a chain around the poles and easily pulled them out of the ground. In less than an hour, all the remaining nine poles were removed.

$\sim$

HOMECOMING

My tour of duty was up on December 17, 1955, so I would have to leave Korea by December 1. I decided to trick my parents and surprise them by coming home sooner than they expected. Before leaving Korea I wrote a series of letters to be mailed by my buddies at three-day intervals after I sailed for home. The letters said my ship was delayed, I missed a shipment, and other reasons why I would be delayed. I called them from the discharge center, after being discharged 10 days early, for them to come and pick me up. They were really surprised because the day before they had received one of my letters saying I was just sailing from Korea. It was a great reunion, and mother prepared the biggest and best steak I have ever eaten. I was home and free from the army forever. These are the things I remember.

During my 720 days in the Army I grew even stronger in my faith, became more self-confident, learned 12 things, and, in a small way, accomplished something significant by protecting the South Koreans from the evil of North Korea. I helped ensure that the death of 33,600 Americans was not in vain because they had made the world a better place. During the 50 years since 1 left there, the South Koreans have become a world economic power, the people have a good standard of living, they enjoy freedom and they have become a Christian nation. North Koreans live in fear, are starving, and live in the darkness of Communistic atheism. What a contrast.

Adventures

CHAPTER VII

My Business Career
.... as I Remember it

Honesty is the first chapter in the book of wisdom.
— Thomas Jefferson

Even as a young boy, I always wanted to be a successful businessman. In bed at night I would fantasize about building a business. My high school year book referred to me as a future businessman. It prophesied that within ten years I would be "A business executive having an office all his own. He also would have a secretary to answer his ringing phone" which came true. I graduated from college with a degree in Business with a major in Finance and a minor in Economics. During my high school years I was pressured to go into Christian service, but always felt that I could be a more effective witness in business. That decision cost me two years of my life because I could not get a deferment from the draft. All of my friends took deferments, but none ended up in the ministry. My belief was that God would honor my hard work and commitment to him with advancement and the compensation to match, and he did.

SERVICE MASTER

I REMEMBER my first day at work as a sixteen year old. My father had arranged for me to work for Wade Wenger & Associates, a company owned by a close family friend, Marion Wade. This company would become Service Master, a five hundred million dollar operation. **This was Breakthrough No. 1.**

My job was filling bottles with various chemicals to be used by crews going on location carpet cleaning. I would work there after school and during school breaks for almost ten years. It was a good source of funds for spending money and college expenses. At first I was in the shop filling bottles, then promoted into working in the rug cleaning plant, and then out with crews doing carpet cleaning in people's homes and businesses.

At the rug cleaning plant, rugs were brought in and put through a vacuum machine, then through a scrubbing machine and finally lifted on poles into a drying room located on the second floor. It was hard work pulling the rugs from machine to machine, but the dangerous part was lifting the rugs with a hoist in the drying room two stories high where a hook on the pole would jump off onto a track. You had to watch very carefully because occasionally the jump did not work and the pole and rug would fall two stories. Down below, the only safe place was behind a large cement post, if you could get there fast enough. (This was before OSHA.) Going into homes to clean carpets was more interesting but hard work moving furniture.

After college I was offered an office job with the company, but my interests were elsewhere.

BELL & HOWELL

After graduating from college I began looking for a job. Initially I looked into the banking and brokerage industries but could not find a satisfactory opening at the level of pay I wanted.

Breakthrough No. 2 came when my cousin's husband arranged an interview for me at Bell & Howell Company. I was hired as a Budget Analyst, and it set the course of my career in industry rather than finance. In hindsight, that

At the beginning, analyzing budgets for Bell & Howell.

was a good thing. It was a great job because of valuable
experiences and the people I interacted with people like
Chuck Percy, Peter P. Peterson, Jack Latter and Bill Roberts,
who were all smart and ethical teachers and mentors. It is
said, "Learn from the best," and they were the best. At one
point B & H acquired an electronic firm on the West Coast.
Our internal auditors found $100 entries on the expense
accounts of some salesmen. These were bribes for government contractors. When Chuck Percy learned of this, he
ordered it to stop. When he was told it could cost millions
of dollars of lost sales, he without hesitation said the practice
would stop. I respected him for this because I knew that
integrity comes from the top down. It was an example I
would not forget.

Because my first job was a Budget Analyst, I was at the
operating level and saw the company from the bottom up.

Chuck Percy was the first man under age thirty to be the President of a Fortune 500 Company. Chuck was a strong leader who gave books to his staff to stimulate their thinking skills. Chuck had an iron-handed Executive Vice President, Bill Roberts, who managed the company. Chuck did not spend much of his time at the office and always had a clean desk.

Then the Board of Directors hired Peter G. Peterson, an advertising executive from Mc Cann Erickson Agency, to be President of the company's largest operating division. It was a disaster! He introduced more new products than the engineers and production people could possibly handle and it became a horrible mess. However, after two years he was promoted to corporate Chief Executive Officer and Percy left to become a U.S. Senator. As corporate CEO, Peterson did an outstanding job of leading and went on to be The Secretary of Commerce and then to be the CEO of Lehman Brothers, one of the worlds largest investment banking firms. He was the Chairman of the Council on Foreign Relations and the author of a number of books. He was one of the founders of the Blackstone Group, a private-equity, asset-management and financial-advisory firm that made him a billionaire. He gave one half of it to a foundation to serve as a think tank for economic policy.

At the time it was difficult to understand how the Board of Directors could promote such a failure. However, the Board saw him as an outstanding leader, and his job managing an operating division was a training ground to prepare him for the top job.

As a Budget Analyst I worked with all the departments so I learned a lot about how businesses operate.

My **Breakthrough No. 3** came when I became a member of a three man team to manage the mismanaged Robert Maxwell Company, a wholly owned subsidiary of the company. Bell & Howell had a marketing problem because its only channel of distribution for the sale of its photographic products was through photo specialty stores.

The company needed a marketing strategy to sell to the mass consumer market. Two marketing executives, <u>Robert</u> Kessenbaum and <u>Maxwell</u> Stroge, were set up in offices on Michigan Avenue in Chicago to sell photo products by direct mail to the mass market. The business was an accounting and operational nightmare.

The profit from a given mailing was impossible to determine until the process was complete, sometimes taking three or four years.

The nightmarish process involved:

- Design of mailing material, a fixed cost.
- Mailing of the material, a fixed cost.
- Shipments of products based the response to mailing, resulting in a billing, a variable cost.
- Return of the product from dissatisfied customers.
- Collection of installment payments over two or three years.
- Accounts given to a collection agency.
- Bad-debt write-off for uncollectable accounts.

As you can see, it was an impossible management and accounting situation. To add to the problem, they decided to sell other products like towels and pots and pans with every deal being different. The company learned a costly lesson; you can not turn two marketing-types loose without tight management and financial control. At one point, I wrote off two million dollars because of poor accounting practices. I also found a cash account with $25,000 for payments that could not be matched with the customer records, which caused great frustration when customers did not get proper credit. It was a real challenge to sort things out and regain control, and I learned a lot and received a lot of recognition.

Breakthrough No. 4 came when I was promoted to Manager of General Accounting, my first supervisory position. I supervised the accounting staff and Accounts Payable department. I set all of the company's accounting policy. It was fun negotiating with the C.P.A.'s from the public accounting firm that audited our account. My degree was in finance, the use of accounting records, not accounting practices, so it required creativity.

After eight years with the company a new Controller, Larry Mullinex, was hired from the outside. He was an arrogant guy who brought two hangmen with him. Suddenly I was an outsider. After two years of not really knowing where I stood with him, I decided to resign before I was fired like some of the others. It was time to move on anyway. The day I resigned he called me into his office and for two hours tried to get me to change my mind and stay with the company. I was flattered, but it was too late; I did not trust him. He was terminated a year after I left, but, unfortunately, all of the good people had left. It troubled me that it had taken the company management so long to act.

$$\sim$$

NATIONAL LOCK

I was determined not to end up unemployed, so I entered the job market and had another offer before I resigned. The new job was in Rockford, Illinois with National Lock Company. It was the defining moment for my career and for our family. It was **Breakthrough No. 5.**

I remember taking my family to Rockford on a Sunday afternoon, checking into a motel, and preparing for a Monday morning interview with Keith Blackstone, the Controller of National Lock. When I woke up on Monday morning, I could not talk! I had laryngitis and could barely whisper. I asked Lura to call Keith to set up the interview for another time, but he insisted that I come to his office anyway. How do you interview for a job when you cannot talk? Well, I did it.

He then sent me downtown to the shrink. Since the doctor could not interview me either, he gave me a written test. As soon as he put the test down before me, I knew God was with me. I had given the very same test to prospective employees at B & H, so I not only knew the questions, but all the answers. I did put down a few wrong answers just to avoid any suspicion. Within a week I had the job offer I wanted and with a 40 percent increase in pay to boot. I accepted and our family began a new life in Rockford, Illinois.

As a financial analyst I had a lot of freedom to move around the company. My challenge was to find things that needed fixing without alienating people. It never pays to make enemies, my father told me and I followed his advice. In looking around the company I observed a huge supply of coal used to generate electricity for the manufacturing plant. My analysis showed that we had over a year's supply on hand. Without management intervention, I convinced the Purchasing Manager and the Supervisor of the Power Plant that a ninety day supply was adequate. They got the credit; I earned two friends and a reputation for being helpful. The power plant was an interesting oddity because it was very unusual for a company to generate its own power. I learned a lot about coal. It is not as fungible as you would think as coal needs to come from the same mine to offer the constant heat based on the design of the furnace. Later we would convert from coal to gas/oil. This required the smoke stack to be reduced from 200 feet to 175 feet. A Chicago firm bid only $10,000 to do the job because they had used a small plane

to inspect the stack and believed it to be of brick construction. Once on the job they discovered that the construction
was brick veneer with a solid concrete core. They had
workers standing on the rim of the stack 200 Feet above
the ground with jackhammers removing the concrete one
inch at a time. They lost a significant amount on the job
but never asked to re-negotiate the contract.

∽

One of the challenges of being in a new company is
how to call management's attention to yourself while making friends. One day I was called into the office of John
Kraman, Vice President of Manufacturing. He had a large
and impressive office with an imposing kidney shaped
desk, a brown leather captain's chair that swiveled like
a merry-go-round, a row of comfortable guest chairs, a
massive green leather couch, two walnut tables with tall
Steifel lamps that spread beams of light and dark shadows
across the room onto the walls and ceiling. It was more
spacious than the President's office. It was the seat of
power with most of the two thousand employees reporting
to this V.P. In a few years this would be my office and I
would sit behind that desk, but at the time it seemed
completely out of reach.
        The vice president and I discussed a number of things
including the employment climate in Rockford. He said
that there was a severe shortage of skilled workers so he
could not hire good people nor increase production. John
was a domineering personality, so no one ever told him he
was wrong. Well I did, and with an angry look on his face
he asked me why. From my snooping around the company,
I knew that the employment office had a sign on the outside door saying: "Applications only accepted 10 AM till
noon and 1 PM to 3." Therefore, skilled workers who were
already employed could not even get into the door to
apply. Because I had stood up to him, he smiled, and John

and I were friends. The Personnel Manager got hell.

The next thing I did was conduct an extensive analysis of the company's profitability. The accounting system was worthless as a management tool, so I designed a format that gave insight into the relative profitability of various business units. When I presented my large red notebook to the President, Chuck Holzwarth, he leaped on it like a tiger after red meat. He formed a committee, called the Basic Business Committee. I was a key member, and it developed into the driving force for decision making for the next 15 years. Over time, we structured business units into product lines – Chair Controls, Casters, Door Locks, Continuous hinges, Cabinet Locks, Packaged Fasteners – and into manufacturing processes – Zinc Die Casting, Injection Molded Plastic Parts, Metal Stamped Parts, Extruded Plastic Parts. We then promoted key people to be Business Managers with responsibility for sales, production and profits. Over the years many of these businesses would be spun-off to other cities like Sikeston, Missouri; Spartanburg and Mauldin, South Carolina; Manitowoc, Wisconsin; Waverly, Tennessee; Waterloo, Canada, and Mexico City, Mexico. With each move it became easier to manage the remaining businesses and weaken the unions strangle- hold on us. Chuck Holzwarth was a great boss. He was a graduate of M.I.T and Harvard Graduate School of Business, a very astute businessman, very loyal to his employees, ethical, a great mentor, and over the years, a good friend. I learned from the best.

Keith Blackstone, the Controller, and I went to a seminar on making visual presentations in Chicago. As we drove back to Rockford, I commented to Keith that, after a full day of listening to the speaker, I had not learned anything new. Then I had an "ah-hah" experience and realized the simple things I had learned would be very useful and I would use them for the rest of my business life.

What did I learn? That the environment of the room was critical; including the size of the room, the temperature, the lighting and the seating arrangement and that visuals pique attention, so they need to be ready for action. Nothing loses attention more quickly than a projector that does not work or is out of focus. I tried to apply my learning, so at my next presentation I went to the room and prepared it for maximum effectiveness, and then returned to my office to review my presentation. As I was returning to the room just before the time of the meeting, I met the man in charge of the meeting in the hallway. He informed me that he had to re-arrange the chairs in the room because they were not in their usual pattern!

After two years with the company, Keith Blackstone, the Controller, left the company for bigger and better things, and I was promoted to Controller and an officer of the company. **Breakthrough No. 6.**

∼

One of the first issues I faced was the company's numbering system for parts which used a generic four digit consecutive number. The number was meaningless unless you knew the part from memory. We had 50,000 raw materials or purchased parts, 100,000 sub-assemblies, and 250,000 finished parts. Because 75% of the workforce had 20 or more years of service I knew massive retirements were pending. Every time a person left, all their knowledge of the parts and processes left with them. Something had to done.

I attended a seminar in Florida where I learned about the Brush-Burn numbering system. It is a system of giving parts a significant number whereby you could look at a part and figure out what the number should be, or look at a number and be able to describe what the part looks like. It was the answer to our problem but had one serious drawback; it took 15 digits to cover all the variations in our parts inventory and the average human mind can only handle a maximum of seven digits. I had a room-full of engineers writing product process sheets. When the information went through the computer program any error would cause it to drop out and all of the information that was downstream would also drop out. This resulted in long lists of dropouts each day. It took over a year for all information to be loaded into the computer.

I encountered another problem: the financial statements had no credibility, so there were lots of excuses for poor performance and no objective basis for decision-making. I remember giving a "something is better than nothing and therefore the statements should be taken at face value until proven otherwise" lecture to the management committee. Once over this hurdle, I combined what I had learned at the seminar on visual presentations with the assistance of a consultant and designed a standardized visual presentation using a graphing system. The Vice President of Sales told me he could now figure out what was happening. When the line is going up, that is good, and when it is going down, that is bad. That may sound simplistic, but it was more effective than looking at rows and columns of numbers. The system was a success and was used by the management committee for years.

❡

One of the problems we had to deal with came with the Executive Order by President Nixon at that time to freeze all prices. This would cripple our company since we were experiencing significant cost inflation, so I was sent to seek relief. I was naïve Mr. Smith going to Washington, D.C., but I soon learned the ways of Washington bureaucrats and began negotiations. I played up to their egos by having our President come to Washington, and we ended up in the bureaucrat's private home one evening pressing the negotiations forward because bureaucrats are so tedious and slow. We played the Midwestern naive image to the hilt and got a letter that allowed unlimited price increases. To celebrate my victory, one of the Division Presidents

invited Lura and me to a dinner-dance at the Rockford
Country Club. After a delightful dinner, the President
asked Lura to dance, but she declined by saying she did
not know how to Polka. He replied that he would teach her
and whisked her off to the dance floor. While Lura danced
with the President, I sat at the table with the President's
wife and traded dog stories. We still joke about Lura's
polka-dancing episode.

One day the President called me into his office and
told me to go to Mexico to our subsidiary company
TEMSA and find out what was going on. I asked him
what he meant, and he just repeated, "Find out what is
going on." When I arrived in Mexico City, I began to play
detective. One of the accounting clerks whispered to me,
"Look at the inventory," so I began auditing and soon
found discrepancies. The tally sheet said 77 parts but there
were only 11; another part was 98, when there were only 8.
The inventory numbers were changed to inflate the profit
to cover the losses in other accounts. I went to the head
office of the Public Accounting firm that audited our
company and confronted the chief CPA with the problem.
He was skeptical because all the accounting records were
kept in a locked truck. We placed the tally sheets up to the
glass windows, and with the light we could see where a
heavier grade of pencil had been used to make 11 into 77
and a 9 placed in front of 8. I gathered further evidence of
inflated expense reports and other fraud. Next, we lured
the President of TEMSA to come to the Mexico City office
of our company attorney where we confronted him. At
first he denied everything, but as the attorney laid out the
evidence I had collected he finally confessed to everything.
We offered to drop the charges if he would resign, but he
tried to blackmail us by claiming no Mexican Court would
side with us because we were a U.S. company and he was

married to a Mexican national. He also knew that if he was terminated, he would receive severance pay from the company worth more than he had stolen. The attorney left the room to prepare the papers to charge him with the crime. I initiated a friendly conversation and discovered he was an alcoholic and was penniless. I offered to pay out his Profit Sharing immediately if he would resign. The prospect of immediate cash was just too enticing for him to decline. I yelled down the hall to the attorney to stop the paperwork, and when he returned I told him of the decision. After he signed the resignation papers, and I returned to Rockford to report what went on.

∾

VICE PRESIDENCY

One day while working with the President in his office, Tom McCullough, who was then a talented V.P. of Manufacturing, interrupted us to say he was not feeling well and was going home. Chuck commented to me how unusual it was because Tom was never sick. Tom died unexpectedly three days later at age 42.

The President and I decided that we would take our time and find a good engineering-type to replace Tom. Within two weeks the manufacturing operation was falling apart. Tom was a manager who made all the decisions and had a staff who could carry out his orders. Tom was an effective manager but not a leader. Organizations can run well with managers in charge but do not run well when they are not present to make decisions. Managers do not empower people like leaders.

At that time I was the Controller of the company and an unlikely choice to become the Vice President of Manufacturing, but because of the urgency of the situation and my leadership skills, I was promoted despite my lack of manufacturing experience. I now sat in the office I

**A relaxed moment for the new Vice President
of Manufacturing at National Lock.**

thought was out of reach, had the key to the executive
restroom and the best executive parking spot. It was an
adrenalin rush, but I was humbled by the thought that
Chuck Holzwarth had put so much faith in me and now
two thousand families were depending on my judgment.
It was **Breakthrough No. 7.**

I began to think and plan on a 13-week horizon, not on
the week-by-week management style of Tom. I went to a
seminar in California to gain an understanding of electro-
plating so I could give direction to something I knew
nothing about. I trained the staff to be decisionmakers
instead of order-takers. I successfully led the manufacturing function for eight years, without any manufacturing
background, based on the belief that if people are given
the tools and authority they need to do the job, know what
is expected, and are coached on how to go about it, they

will perform better than expected. This proved to be right.

The first item on my action plan was a new Production & Inventory system. The present system was like a meat grinder you launched a production order at one end, cranked, the finished product came out the end, and no one knew what was going on inside the grinder. The customer order "shipped-complete- and-on time" record was 60%. I hired a consultant to advise on how to use state-of-the-art computer programs. It was now possible because we had a good parts-numbering program in place and because computers were now powerful enough to handle the immense amount of data required. The new system worked great because we now knew where every order was in the process and could expedite or delay parts while in process based on the customers' ever-changing requirements. This reduced inventory by 25% and improved the on-time rate to 90%.

⌒⌣

One of the production workers, the wife of a union officer, filed a complaint with the Occupational Health and Safety Commission (OSHA) claiming that the machine she worked at was unsafe. An investigation by an OSHA inspector found the claim unfounded. A few months later, she filed a second complaint which was also found groundless, but since two complaints had been filed, they would do a complete inspection of the whole plant. It was a "set-up."

When OSHA was created it had two choices; judge companies by their safety record or by the physical conditions of their facilities. Every professional in the safety field knew the safety record was the best criteria, but the unions prevailed and the law was passed to inspect and levy fines for conditions that did not comply with regulations. This precipitated thousands of pages of regulations covering everything from the shape of toilet seats and the size of exit signs to machine guarding.

Every professional in the safety field knew that safety training and safety awareness produced better results than

trying to provide a safe environment. We had an
exceptionally good safety record based on lost days off
due to accidents vs. hours worked . Here is an illustration
of this fact. In our Die Casting Department we had an
accident when one of our workers got his arm caught in
a closing of two dies. Tragically, his arm and hand were
squeezed into the shape of a Swedish pancake by the die-
closing pressure of 250,000 tons per square inch. This
seemed impossible because the machine had a door that
closed, covering the total entrance to the die cavity, and
the machine is triggered to close only when the door is
completely shut. When the machine was open he had
reached into the die cavity to remove a hung-up part, a
violation of the safety rules, and when he reached into
the die area he pushed the activating switch with his body.
Inspection of the accident scene revealed that he had pried
the cover off the box that contained the switch in order to
cycle the machine faster and increase his production and
his pay. The lesson to be learned from this: While providing a safe environment is essential, safety training and
awareness is the only way to have a good safety record.

∽

In the 70-year-old plant, the OHSA inspector had no
problem finding violations, and we received a long report
citing numerous deficiencies and substantial fines. The
fines were bad enough, but the cost of correcting the
problem would cost millions.

I decided on a strategy of nit-picking the citation to
death and called in our safety expert and an attorney from
Chicago with OSHA experience. Armed with lots of
points, I called the OSHA headquarters and requested a
two day review with the regional director. The secretary
who took my call said that no one ever needed more than
two hours of the busy director's time, but I insisted. We

started a detailed review of the complaint, discussing the difference between rotates and revolves– the earth rotates around the sun and revolves around its axis. One part of the citation referred to point "ii," which was an error. I suggested it should have been "iv," a minor item, but I think they really meant "vi" a major expense item. He accepted my suggestion and we moved on to a subject of major disagreement.

Out of the corner of my eye, I picked up on a sign from my safety expert. I took a chance and inferred that we knew more about the subject than he did and called upon my man to explain. He said, "On about page 329 of the manual there is a diagram and material that covers the point in question." What the director did not know was that my expert had a photographic memory, and when he opened the manual, there it was just as he had described it. At this point the director gave up, privately complaining that we were the most contentious SOB's he had ever encountered, and agreed to withdraw the complaint and issue a revised one.

On a return visit to the OSHA headquarters, we were caught in a great snowstorm and were marooned for two days, taking shelter with a family in their country-side home. I phoned the OSHA director and explained our situation and asked for an extension for a review of the revised citation. He stated that the law was clear and that no extensions were permitted. Again, I out-maneuvered him, citing that the complaint was not signed by the right official and therefore was invalid. He collapsed, and we ended up with a short list of minor things to correct and minimal fines. We out- OSHA'd OSHA by using the same game they used against us, against them, and WON!

**A handshake but no deal. That's me on the right,
and a man who was trying to sell National Lock a
device that he claimed could break into one of the
company's high-security locks. The offer, suspected
to be fraudulent, was turned down.**

As the Vice President of Manufacturing I had many
interesting experiences. One day I received a phone call
from a man who wanted to sell me his device for breaking
into one of our high- security locks. He was a crook who
had spent his idle hours in prison figuring out how to break
our lock, and now he wanted to cash in by extorting money
from us, the manufacturer. This was a serious problem
because our locks were installed in vending machines
all over the county. We began getting reports of vending
machines being broken into and the money in the lock box
being stolen. I decided to play along with him to entrap
him.   I invited him to come to Rockford from Tennessee
to make a deal. We arranged for a breakfast meeting at the
Sweden House Restaurant adjoining the Sweden House

Motel. I had our security man, a former police officer, stationed at the motel the night before our planned meeting. When a man arrived with a Tennessee license plate our security man trailed him into the motel. The first the thing the crook did was to case the place by checking every exit door, elevator and stairwell in the motel. The next morning we arrived early for the meeting and sat at a table in the restaurant to plan our strategy before he came. When the appointed time came he did not show up, so we had our breakfast and continued to discuss our strategy knew the law required the extortionist to state a specific amount of money in order to charge him with a crime. When we finished breakfast a man, the crook, came over from an adjoining table and introduced himself. He had been close enough to overhear our conversation.

Our strategy was to get him to tell us the amount he wanted. I tried to draw him out to tell us an amount he wanted a number of times but each time he would not directly give me an amount. He knew the law and without his requesting a given amount we had no case. I have a photograph of our parting handshake. Our engineers redesigned our lock. I learned you can't out smart a crook, they know their business better than you.

After eight years, longer than any job I had ever had, time was running out. Foreign imports were gaining a significant market share.

We had already moved many operations out of Rockford to avoid the union's tight grip and wages and benefits that were way above the competition. Some serious thought was needed as to what should be done next.

Chuck Holzwarth asked me to become a V.P. of Strategic Planning. Since the union would not give an inch, we decided to shut the Rockford plant down. It was a very difficult decision. The U.A.W. won and the workers lost.

KEYSTONE CONSOLIDATED INDUSTRIES

About this time, our corporate parent, Keystone Consolidated Industries, located in Peoria, Illinois, hired a new corporate CEO, George Arnold, the first nonfamily CEO in its history. He noticed the strategic planning I was doing in Rockford and was impressed. He offered me a Corporate VP job. I was to be an extension of his office and have an office right next to his. I would have the most influence on all his decisions. This was **Breakthrough No. 8.**

I accepted the offer and in September, 1979 began to commute. Commuting was pleasant because I could fly from Rockford to Peoria where a chauffeur would take me to my office, but being away from home so much was depressing. Needless to say, there was a lot of jealousy with the present staff and even family members who had been passed up. Everything was going well until five

I accepted an offer from George Arnold, left, the new CEO, to join him at Keystone. I am on the right.

months later when the CEO abruptly resigned and left the
company without explanation. I had lost my sponsor and
the new CEO was a family member. I was not loved.

I developed a strategic plan for the entire corporation.
It was to be presented to the Board of Directors for their
approval. Since this was a special meeting of the Board,
we decided to keep it confidential from the employees and
the press by renting a room at a local hotel. When we
arrived at the hotel there on the marquee for the entire
world to see was, "Welcome Keystone Board." My plan
was approved by the Board, and since it was my idea,
much of the implementation was assigned to me. I was
to oversee the restructuring through acquisition, expansion,
sale or closure of various business units.

I had a diverse group of operations reporting directly
to me: a research center developing a low-coefficient-
of-friction material, the world's largest producer of hog
houses, a machine shop making precision equipment
for the strapping industry, and Life Time Gate, a farm
gate manufacturing company. This diversity helped me
broaden my base of experience and would be valuable
for my future. Since these businesses were all located in
different cities, I traveled a lot.

Another responsibility I had was to serve on the
Employee Benefits Committee of the Board of Directors.
As a member of the committee I managed the company's
profit sharing and pension funds. I would select various
Investment Management firms to actually do the investing.
What I discovered was that they all had great investment
records, so it was a matter of selecting firms with different
investment philosophies. One bond manager had a system
that back-tested, showing a long history of how their
system successfully worked. It appeared to be a sure thing,
but after a year of poor results I visited his office in New
York and asked him what had happened to his fool-proof
system. "Oh I gave up on the system months ago," he
reported. His system presentation was just a sales gim-
mick. I fired him and he lost his job with his company.

This experience would be valuable for my future, and I was sure God was preparing me for something significant.

The company and I shared the common belief that training and development were important. One summer I went to Harvard Graduate School near Boston. While I had already studied at seven universities, I found Harvard the most accelerated learning experience of my life. One of the subjects was Anti-Takeover Techniques, so when I returned to the company I met with our CEO to share my knowledge. He assured me everything was already in place. He lied to me, because within a year the company would be taken over by Harold Simmons, a ruthless Texas multi-million-aire. There was no plan in place and the family lost Keystone.

Because of my wide-ranging responsibilities, I commuted a lot.

I have always regretted how I was fooled by this man. He appeared to be a distinguished, wise and thoughtful businessman, puffing on his pipe and being very tight-lipped at meetings, but he turned out to be a cunning, shallow and deceptive man.

After two years of travel and commuting, I was ready for an office in Rockford, and for administrative purposes reported to Dave Sutton. Dave was the Nazi Commandant-type psychopath (no feelings for people and unethical behavior without conscience) who, more than once, tried to intimidate and bribe me, but I resisted. I had worked with Dave for years and he knew about my Christian faith, so I was disappointed with the fact that he thought I could be bribed. In due time, as with most people like him, he was terminated. It was company policy to have a neutral party present during the termination to be a witness. Dave and his boss, Chuck Holzwarth, both agreed on a third party - guess who? During the termination meeting I was more than an observer, participating in the give and take to make sure Dave got fair treatment. Because of my integrity Dave wanted me to be present during this humiliating experience, so maybe my Christian witness did matter.

∽

After 17 years with the company I felt it was time to move on because I was tired of always doing what other people wanted me to do. It was a difficult decision because I had a good and dependable salary and benefits. In a meeting with a select few we were assured by the new owner, Harold Simmons, that we would always have a meaningful job somewhere in his organization, even if National Lock was closed down. My instincts told me not to believe him, and they were confirmed later when everyone in the room eventually was terminated. He offered me a job at his corporate headquarters in Dallas, but I had no interest in working with him because he was an asset manipulator rather than asset builder, and I was a builder.

Over a period of two years I had been thinking about having my own business. People had always sought my advice, but I did not know if they where willing to pay for it. I resigned from National Lock and founded ROBERT LAWRENZ CONSULTING SERVICES, INC. I chose the name because the company would be me, and I was uncertain whether the services would be personal, business or both. When I gave Chuck Holzwarth my resignation I was without even one client, so it was done on pure faith. God had always been with me, so why would he forsake me now? My faith was rewarded a few days later when Chuck came into my office and said that the work I was doing at National Lock needed to be done, and I was the only qualified person to do it, so he offered to be my first client. Before I was even out the door, I had a six-month contract and cash flow. I knew God was in charge of my life. It was **Breakthrough No. 9 and a defining moment in our lives.**

❦

ROBERT LAWRENZ CONSULTING SERVICES

Going into business for myself could not have been a better fit for me.

All the essentials were in place: A deep desire to help people be the best and have the very best for lives, which is one of my core values A record of building long-term relationships, being honest and trustworthy to keep confidences. An expertise in strategy and planning. Good skills with both people and numbers. Extensive experience in both investments and business. An entrepreneurial bent. I kept confidences, even from Lura, so when we were both talking with clients at social events they would assume I had shared their story with her and were amazed, and somewhat relieved, to find out how tight-lipped I was.

Over two years of thinking and planning for my new business, I came up with the idea of a personal and business financial advisory service that would charge for services on a fee basis rather than on commissions. My problem was that there were no businesses like that to be a good model for me.

About that time there were six people sitting in a hotel room in Kansas City trying to figure out how to do financial planning on a fee-only basis. This emerged into an organization called The National Association of Personal Financial Planners which I eventually found and became a member. This was very helpful because everyone was willing to share their expertise. It became the leading trend for the whole financial industry with commissioned brokers all becoming Financial Advisors, so my timing was perfect. People never really trusted their broker; he seemed to sit on the other side of the table from them while planners sat beside them. In my new work I learned to never swim up-stream. I wanted to honor the Lord by donating 10 percent of my time to those who could not afford me. At times it would be a lot more than 10 percent, but the Lord always provided enough paying business for me to be able to do this.

I started the business with a downtown office shared with two attorneys to keep my overhead low. National Lock and Elco Industries were two of my first corporate accounts, and my first personal planning client was one that Lura referred to me. Since the wife wore outdated dresses, Lura told me not to charge very much. You guessed it; they had more money than we did.

Over the years I would serve over 100 clients and manage over $100,000,000 in client assets. Truly the Lord blessed.

Next, I set up my own office in the Last Straw Building and hired my first female employee. I am not a chauvinist, but I never had a female employee who was satisfactory in my years of being in business. The first, after I had trained her for two years, left. The next one was a mother with a pre-school child who I hired because her husband worked nights and could care for a sick child while she worked. Shortly after I hired her, she divorced and took lots of time off to care for her child. After five years when her child started school and most of the childhood diseases were over, she quit. Next, there was a young college graduate who did not work out and had to be terminated.

Wendy, a middle-aged woman, was a very proficient employee, but her attendance was erratic. She needed a lot of time off work for doctor visits, tests and treatments for an array of physical problems. She would come to work on Monday morning looking like she gone through hell over the weekend, eyes sunken and unfocused, face taunt and pale, lips tight, and a countenance that revealed death would be a reprieve. She had eventually confided in me that as a young girl she was sexually molested by her uncle and had married a physically and sexually abusive husband.

After a while I became suspicious that there was more going on than just physical problems and referred her to a psycho-therapist I knew who specialized in dealing with evil spirits. As part of her therapy she was to read the book Bondage Breakers. One night as she was preparing to go to bed and read the book, the book flew across the room, as if under its own power, but it was the spirit who was threatened and did not want her to read the book. During an exorcism, the spirit was asked for his name and her uncle's voice came out of her mouth, she was talking but the words were not hers. After the exorcism she was a new person, her physical problems melted away and she became a happy well-adjusted person. It was personally rewarding to know I had been God's agent to change another life. Then, there was a more mature woman for whom the job was too challenging, and I had to terminate her after a few months.

Fortunately, all the men I hired worked out very well. Fred Raffety joined me after working for 20 years as a trust officer in several banks. He had a law degree, a great deal of experience in investing and was a perfect fit. While

I was the optimist and could always see how things could work out, Fred was the realist. When we were conferring on a decision, I had to force myself to listen to him because he was usually right. He gave good advice, such as avoiding packaged investment products, keeping it simple with stocks, bonds and mutual funds and changing our fee structure to a percentage of assets managed. He saved me a lot of pain and our client's lots of money. I treated Fred like an equal partner and our mutual respect grew. We became friends. He eventually bought the business from me. As the business grew we moved to a larger office on East State Street and then moved further east to a new office building with convenient parking. Each move was to a little bigger and nicer facility than the previous one. We wanted to portray an image of nice and comfortable, but not plush.

$\sim$

PERSONAL PLANNING CLIENTS

The personal financial planning clients made the effort the most rewarding and meaningful for me. Almost every client responded to the goal setting we helped develop. Goals are the ultimate dream and most of our clients were very capable people. Once the goals were clear, they could make them happen with coaching from us. Our approach was to help the client sort out what made life meaningful, stated in the form of "Life Goals." The goals ranged from buying a boat and sailing the Caribbean to having space to plant a garden. Both came true. Once the life goals were in place we created an action plan and then a financial plan to support their goals. Many of our clients originally came to us to help them get rich, but hopefully found that real meaning in life comes from relationships, experiences and personal fulfillment.

$\sim$

One client couple was referred by another client for whom we had successfully sold his business and were managing his portfolio. When Rodney and Shelly came to me, we worked on their Life Goals. These were their ultimate dreams: sell his business, buy a boat to sail the Caribbean for six months out of the year and travel around the United States by RV for the other six months. They both loved to sail and Rodney had a strong interest in U.S. history, especially the Civil War, so travel to the east and south where high on his list. After we had the life goals in writing, we began implementation. I was commissioned to sell the business and found a family who wanted to buy it. The father who had a strong personality, who was not acceptable to the sellers because of the methods he would use with their employees. He claimed he wanted to buy the business for his son and retire. The son was a capable engineer but under the control of his father. We were fooled into believing him, and after the sale, the father ran the business which meant all the key managers left within a year.

As part of the sale negotiations, Rodney received a three-year employment agreement, which permitted him to sail for six months and work for six months. After two years he wanted out of the contract because the father was so unreasonable. I negotiated him out of the deal. After the sale, Rodney and Shelly bought a 42' sail boat in Boston that needed to be completely refitted. They worked on it for six months and then sailed it down the intercoastal waterway to Florida and then on to the Caribbean. Their first three goals of their life plan were accomplished, and their dream had come true.

During the next few years, tragedy would strike three times which would weigh heavily on their emotional state. First, their oldest son, who had moved to Chicago, committed suicide. On the phone with Shelly, I could not determine her mental state, so I asked her how he died. "He hanged himself," she confided in me. This answer gave me insight into her mental state - she was coherent.

Rodney believed in God, but that was it. Shelly was a scoffer, so offering words of comfort were difficult. The funeral was in a church but lacked a clear Christian message. Urging them to think back on all the good times they had enjoyed together was the best comfort I could offer.

When the next tragedy occurred, Rodney called me on the phone and said, "I have done the worst thing possible." All kinds of things raced through my mind as he told me his story. He and Shelly lived in Northern Illinois and planned to go to Belwood, Iowa, for breakfast. While it is a very short distance, Rodney decided to fly his Piper plane stationed in the Rockford Airport to the Belwood Airport – mistake number one. Since it was such a short flight, Rodney did not file a flight plan with the FAA nor did he check with his map book - mistakes number two and three. He flew to the Belwood Airport and landed on a snow-packed runway – mistake number four. The snow covered a large white "X" painted on the runway to indicate the airport was closed. As he taxied his plane he was preoccupied with looking for Shelly who had driven to the airport - mistake number five. Suddenly, there was a woman walking her dog standing right in his path. Rodney tried to stop the plane but it was too late and he hit her with the wing of the plane - mistake number six. While the plane was only traveling at about three miles per hour, the blow knocked her down and broke her back. She was a paraplegic and would be helpless for the rest of her life. Rodney was emotionally devastated.

I immediately went to their home and tried to comfort them with the explanation that, like many freak accidents, six mistakes all in sequence was a statistical impossibility. It was a true accident and was not intentional, nor was there gross negligence on his part. As we sat together, I held Shelly's hand and prayed with them for God's forgiveness, their comfort and for the injured woman. It was a very touching moment and I felt their grief. While I asked for their permission to pray, later Shelly in her bitterness would resent it because of her anger with God.

The injured family decided to play hardball and sued for $1.4 million. The first $1 million would be paid by the insurance company, but the balance would be Rodney's responsibility. At my recommendation, Rodney hired a personal attorney because the insurance company had no interest in fighting the claim. It was clearly Rodney's fault and the claim far exceeded their limit. After lengthy negotiations we offered $1.15 million and they demanded $1.175 million. Since I had just made $25,000 in Rodney's investments the prior month, and Rodney and Shelly were at the emotional breaking point, I recommended we settle at their demand level, so Rodney called his attorney and told him to settle. It was Friday and the injured person's attorney was out of his office but returned the call over the weekend. Our attorney decided not to return the call until Monday because he was going out of town. On Sunday the woman unexpectedly died. The claim was quickly settled for $700,000.

The final tragedy was their middle son who became hopelessly addicted to drugs and alcohol and, therefore, could not hold a job but somehow came up with the rent money each month. On my recommendation, we retained the services of a professional who assisted in an intervention program. I was asked to participate and met in a hotel room to be briefed on the process with other friends and family. We knew he had guns, so it was dangerous, but we proceeded to his home and met him at the front door. This was the third time I put my life in the hands of God. The son would not let us in and threatened to shoot us, so the police were called and he was arrested and taken to jail. The next morning Rodney bailed him out of jail, but after that the son had little contact with his parents and eventually died from a suicidal overdose. This would weigh heavily on them. They had a third son who lived in Colorado and had his act together, which was a great comfort to them.

Rodney and Shelly had everything going for them except for one thing. They loved each other and their

children, they were good moral people, they were good
citizens, they had financial success, but they had no faith
or trust in God. I had done all I could do for them. I managed their finances and helped them realize their dreams.
I stood by them throughout the tragedies they experienced,
comforting and wisely advising them but without God
in their lives, life was truly meaningless, and they had
nothing to give their children except money. Because
there was little hope, they became depressed and paranoid.
Life without God's assurances and the inner strength
he provides sometimes makes life unbearable.

$$\sim$$

Next I will tell you about a story of another client
who confronted challenges just as difficult as Rodney's
and Shelly's, but tapped God's resources and has a story
book ending.

This is a true story of a severely broken person who was
able to return to normal life because of her trust in God.
It took many years and with the help of my encouragement
and mentoring, and the help of a number of caring
Christian friends. Remember, I am a "fee only" financial
planner who offers 10% of my time to mentor those who
cannot afford my services. Teresa was one of these people.

Teresa sat in my office, a completely broken person.
She looked down, her shoulders bent over and leaning
forward like a weeping willow tree. She was physically
and emotionally destroyed. She had just divorced her third
husband and made a number of bad decisions. She was a
new Christian, but her faith was being tested. Her former
spouse was a controlling and abusive husband who continued to try to control, intimidate, humiliate and harass her
for many months. She feared for her life. He manipulated
her two sons into hating their mother. I accepted her as
a client not fully realizing what was ahead.

I assessed the situation and found she had no employment or source of income for herself or for child support payments or medical expenses for her two boys. Neither did she have custody rights or any assets except for the clothes on her back and an aging car with monthly payments. She also had $100,000 in debt that reverted back to her because her ex-husband declared bankruptcy. Her attorney had sold her out, leaving her with impossible responsibilities for the next 10 years, and, in effect, keeping her under the control of her former husband. I prepared a Life Goals Plan with specific goals and we started the recovery process. It was a very long road and lots of hard work, but God continued to work in her life.

The first step was to review her divorce decree. It was a nightmare, written by her former husband, giving him everything and her nothing but impossible obligations. He was to get all the assets, including their home, and sole custody of the children. She would get the clothes on her back, her five-year-old car with a large loan balance, and child support payments, including all medical expenses. When I asked her about the attorney who represented her Teresa said all her attorney did was zoom through the agreement and tell her to sign it. The attorney realized she was no match for Teresa's former husband, even though he was not an attorney, as we would experience with three other attorneys we hired.

The next thing her former husband did was to set her up. He came with their two sons to the house where she was staying and started taking things out of her car. He had the keys which turned out to be a problem as he continued harassing her. When she was lured out of the house, one of her brainwashed sons called her an obscene name, and she instinctively gave him a quick slap on his face. That was all it took; her former husband took her to court and obtained a restraining order which effectively cut her off from all contact with her sons, not even a birthday card or a phone call was allowed. I told her to be very patient and the boys would eventually figure things out and she would

regain her relationship with them, which finally did
happen.

God cared for her through a Christian couple who
gave her good spiritual counsel and encouragement, and
another Christian friend who gave her a place to live, so
she did not have to live on the street.

The next step in her Life Goals action plan was to find
employment. While visiting a friend at the local hospital,
she decided to stop by the Employment Department of the
hospital and ask for an application. She knew there were
no job openings for nurses but wanted her application on
file in case there was an opening. When she completed the
application, the Personnel Manager said that she thought
there was an opening and she could interview right then.
Teresa tried to postpone the interview because she did not
have her resume nor was she dressed appropriately, but the
manager persisted. She got the job with good pay and
much needed benefits. However, on her third day of work,
her supervisor told her that they had a made mistake.
There was no vacancy, but they would keep her on anyway. It was a God Thing.

The next step was to get her finances under control.
Under the terms of her divorce decree, she had to pay child
support and medical expenses for her two boys, ages 12
and 14, which she was willing to do to keep the boys in
their home. With her salary and benefit plan, the cost
was manageable.

The divorce agreement provided for her ex-husband
to get all the assets and debt, except for one car with a
loan, but he declared bankruptcy and all the $100,000 debt
reverted to her. I hired a Rockford attorney and we filed in
the Northern Illinois District Bankruptcy Court using my
Rockford address to prevent her former husband from
finding out and objecting. It is common practice for the
court attorney to ask if the person filing has been a resident
of the district for at least six months to be eligible. God
was in control, and the attorney did not ask that question.
Once all the debt was cleared, she was on her way to

independence. The next step was to stop the harassment.

While at work her car was unprotected in an open parking lot. Once her ex-husband slashed her tires, which cost her money she did not have to replace them. Another day he put a stink bomb in her car and disabled the electric windows so she could not even air out the car. On another occasion, he came to the lobby of the Hilton Hotel during a hospital fund-raising dinner and began yelling at her in front of everyone to embarrass her. He sent letters to her, trying to control her by demanding things even though they were no longer married. One letter was doused in perfume which we feared was designed to cover up some toxic substance, so I kept it in a sealed plastic envelope. Over the years he would go on the attack by taking her to court where he would represent himself so he did not have any legal expense, but she did. We hired three different lawyers but each one was outwitted by her ex-husband. Eventually he met his match when her new father-in-law, who was a partner in a prestigious Chicago law firm but not a family practice lawyer, won in court. The order of protection was allowed to expire and that was the end of the legal harassment.

Now things were going well for Teresa. She had a good solid job in her chosen field and an adequate income and benefits to pay the child support. Finding a place where she could live on her own was challenging because of her poor credit rating. Spiritually, she was maturing, and attending regular Bible studies with her mentor. One day at work, a fellow employee told her that one of the maintenance men had expressed an interest in meeting her. After three failed marriages, she was in no mood to get involved with a man. Daniel asked her to go on a short walk with him, and she agreed to that. Six months later they were walking down the aisle of a church.

Daniel was the perfect match – caring, loving and with just the temperament to handle a strong-willed woman. He had been raised in a Catholic home but was turned off by religion. Daniel became a born-again Christian and matured rapidly under the mentoring of a friend.

∽

   While the marriage was going well, she became increasingly dissatisfied with her work situation. She was a registered nurse but did not have a degree in nursing, and therefore had limited opportunity for advancement. I advised her to go back to school and get a degree, which she did and graduated with honors. That did enable her to get a better, more rewarding and a higher paying job in a doctor's office. After a few years, she found the patient work was very rewarding, but her supervisor was a very disagreeable woman. I advised her to once again go back to school and become a Nurse Practitioner. She again graduated with honors and was able to get an even better and more satisfying job with better pay.

   Today she is a complete person. She has a loving relationship with her new godly husband, a meaningful job with a 6 figure income, a beautiful home in the suburbs, and a restored relationship with her children. She, under the Spirit's leading, even reconciled with her former husband. She is active in her church and is outspoken about her faith in the goodness of God. She says, "Those Life Goals kept me focused."

∽

CORPORATE PLANNING CLIENTS

   Corporate clients would be referred to us because their business was in trouble. We were very good at sorting out the problem and helping get things back on track. Once the problem was solved, we would look forward to continuing the relationship to enjoy the fun part of growing their business. You would think we would have earned their confidence and good will, but as soon as the pressure was

off, every one of them cut us off. You have to understand the psyche of the entrepreneur to understand this
phenomenon. Ego is the very trait that made them business
owners to begin with. By the time they came to us they
had already exhausted every option and we were their last
resort. Once the problem is solved, their ego kicked in and
they felt no need for any assistance. Some returned to their
former way of doing business and crashed.

Gerald came to me and asked me to audit his books.
One Saturday morning I went to his office and quickly
discovered discrepancies in his accounting system. I put
on my detective hat. His accountant kept telling him to
increase the volume of business and his cash flow problem
would be solved. Gerald kept increasing business, but his
cash flow problem became even worse.

The accountant, Cal Lighthall, had all the books and
records at his office that were needed for evidence. We
arranged for Gerald to break into Cal's office at night.
Lura, Gerald's wife Carol, and I sat in a local restaurant
while Gerald did the break-in. While we were sitting there,
a police squad car came flying by with its siren screeching,
and we were fearful that Gerald had been discovered.
Fortunately, the police were on another call. When Gerald
returned, he had all the books and I advised him not to
keep the records at his office, so he kept them in the
trunk of his car.

A few days later, Gerald went to his office and when
he opened the door he smelled the strong odor of gas.
Fortunately he did not flick on the lights because the spark
could have caused a massive explosion that could have
leveled the building and killed Gerald. During the night,
his office had been broken into and the safe forced open.
It was a large safe that contained some cash, but nothing
had been removed, so the robbers were apparently looking
for the books. The intruders had also broken the pipe in
the furnace to allow the gas to flow.

My investigation of Cal revealed mafia connections in
Chicago, so he was a dangerous guy. What I discovered

was an elaborate Ponzi Scheme his accounting firm was using. He told his clients to reimburse him for taxes he paid on their behalf. He did not pay the taxes, pocketed the money and had the delinquency notices sent directly to his office so the client was unaware of the delinquency. Just before the IRS would come after the first client, the accountant would make payment from funds from a second client, thus perpetuating the scam. We had the evidence, confirmed by police detectives, but the State's Attorney's Office, for reasons we never understood, was reluctant to prosecute. After being pressured by all the victims the State's Attorney went to the Grand Jury and got an indictment, but the State's Attorney was again reluctant to take it to trial even though he had a solid case.

We created public pressure on him to take the case to trial by generating press releases about the "alleged" crimes that I prepared for the local TV stations. I would call the station and ask for the newsroom and give them my spin, which they would take down. Sometimes they complained about the length and I would give them per-mission to edit it, but they were too lazy to do it. I would go home and see my release reported on TV that night just as I had written it. I was amazed at how easy it was; they never verified my story or checked my credentials.

The day of the trial I called the local newspaper, The Rockford Register Star, and asked for the supervisor of news reporters. When I found the right person I asked who would be assigned to cover the big embezzlement trial that day and the response was, "What trial?" I acted surprised that they were unaware of such a major case. "Oh, you are a tipster," was the response.

Before the trial, I patrolled the hallway of the court house until I found a person with one of those 3x9 reporter note pads. I introduced myself and sat next to him in the visitor's gallery. When the defendant was testifying, every time he would lie I would jot a note that the reporter could see, so he could report the truth. When the defendant was on the witness stand, I noticed that every time he lied he

would involuntarily move his right shoulder. I wonder if
the judge noticed it because he found him guilty and
sentenced him to three to five years in jail.

Meanwhile I was instrumental in keeping Gerald out of
personal bankruptcy. Afterward he went through corporate
bankruptcy and re-structured the business. It was exciting,
I got paid, but the business relationship ended as soon as
the problem was solved.

❧

Walter came to me because he was in big trouble.
We had become acquainted while serving on the Board
of Directors of Rockford Christian School. He had the
innate bent to always choose the wrong people to work
for him, so he was under-served, mis-served and conned
repeatedly. He became paranoid. At first he would over-
estimate people's competency, putting them on a pedestal.
Then, once he would catch on to them, he would lose
confidence and finally turn on them with disapproval,
He would turn off the initiative of all his people by getting
personally involved in the detailed decisions and screwing
up everything. The business was founded by his father
and started operating in a chicken coop. There was a
proudly displayed picture of the chicken coop in his office.
His father invented a fastener threading machine that was
unique and provided a flood of orders for years. As a boy,
Walter would tinker with the machines in his father's shop
and developed a talent for mechanical things. So after
serving time in the Air Force, he did not go to college,
but went directly to work for his father. After his father's
death, Walter, his sister Carolyn, and his mother owned
and operated the business. I remember going to a Board of
Directors meeting where Carolyn gave a financial report,
the presentation of which was a time for deciding which
bills should be paid. Mother, who came to the meeting in a

wheelchair, sat staring into space. Walter deeply loved his
mother and sister, and was extremely protective of them.
Despite Walter's business incompetence, the business grew
and expanded because of his mechanical genius. He eventually overextended himself and had to file for bankruptcy.

Walter was not even given "Debtor in Possession"
control, and the business was placed under the control of a
Chicago law firm. Under law, the business in bankruptcy is
to be operated for the benefit of creditors, but, in reality, it
is operated for the benefit of creditors' attorneys. They are
vultures picking meat off the carcass until there is nothing
left but a few dead bones. Then they fly away. The attorneys for the debtor play the same game of protracting the
process to collect bigger fees. Walter was in a perfect
storm, in effect paying one set of attorneys to fight against
him and paying another set of attorneys to defend him.
When he came to me for help, I remember getting all the
attorneys in the same room at the same time and giving
them an ultimatum to get things settled, or else Walter
would walk away and there would be nothing left for them.
Walter had personally invited a Chicago lawyer to come to
the meeting to advise us, but we ended up giving him the
assignment to negotiate with the bankruptcy lawyers.
When I told him he had to settle it for $25,000, he was in
shock but said he would try. He was a securities lawyer
and knew nothing about bankruptcy law, but he did it.
Next we had to get the American Bank, a secured creditor,
to agree to the settlement. When we met with the banker,
we presented the books to demonstrate how the company
could survive. He threw the books on the floor, declaring
they were worthless, but did eventually agree, based on
our reputation. We became miracle workers when we
saved the company, and thereafter the bank referred a
lot of business to us.

After Walter regained control of the business, he was
in our office and we decided to go to lunch together. As
we walked across the parking lot, Walter began to talk in
gibberish. I asked him if he was all right and he clearly

said he was fine, but shortly thereafter it was evident he was having a stroke. At the hospital the doctor said he had bled a lot and recommended surgery.

After surgery, Walter was never the same, and I took over the operation of his company the very next day in addition to my own business. Walter's business after the bankruptcy was not doing well. Sales were just over a million dollars, all the key employees were gone and the business was losing about $100,000 a year. I initiated a number of things: a new accounting and costing system, a production control system, promoted the new Sales Manager to be the President, promoted one of the remaining good employees to Controller, and started holding regular Board of Directors meetings. The new board included Walter as Chairman, his sister Carolyn, and his wife Beatrice and along with Fred Raffety and me as non-family directors. Through my leadership, we were able to turn the business around. In my five years as CEO, sales were up to $6 million dollars, profits to $1 million dollars and we had a strong balance sheet. I had taken Walter's personal net worth from zero to about $5 million dollars.

Everything was going well, but Walter became his old self and became paranoid about the President and Controller. One of Walter's pets was his secretary who acted as a spy and informant. She was not very smart but very cunning. One of her assignments was to record the time women spent in the restroom and report it to Walter. When she failed to follow a direct order of the Controller, her supervisor, he suspended her without pay for three days. She went directly to Walter and he accepted her side of the story, a lie, over the Comptroller's objections, reinstated her pay and made the Controller apologize to her. Without even telling Fred or me, Walter hired one of the company's previous attorneys to be CEO, paying her $250,000 a year. He was conned again.

Fred and I considered the situation carefully because our fees were $75,000 per year, then we jointly decided to resign as Directors. Walter was shocked and wanted us to stay on. How could we when he did not even ask our opinion as Directors before he hired the woman? Fred and I could see nothing but conflict because we knew she would destroy the company. She did, and within fourteen months the doors were shut, the company was back in bankruptcy and Walter's net worth was back to zero.

FOCUS FINANCIAL ADVISORS

After twenty years of the most rewarding work I had ever done, it was time to retire. I had made a commitment to Fred Raffety years before that I would give him first opportunity to buy the business. We came to an agreement without haggling and he took over the business. We renamed the company Focus Financial Advisors and began the transition.

After a wonderful and meaningful retirement party that included a harpist playing in the background and two gifts, a beautiful vase and a portrait of me painted by one of our clients, I took a month's vacation to New Zealand. It was planned so Fred could be in charge without my interference. Now that Fred owned the business, Lura and I implemented our dream of moving to Minnesota to be close to our daughters, son-in-law and grandchildren. With my computer and regular quarterly visits to Rockford, I continued to manage the investments of a select number of clients. This kept me engaged with the people with whom I had developed relationships over the years.

What had I learned? That working can be fun and exciting, that life has meaning by serving others, that planning and goal setting works to accomplish the really important things in life, that measuring things is essential to reaching goals and that combining work and ministry is the perfect combination.

Afterthoughts
CHAPTER VIII

My Personal Observations on Life

Man plans, but God laughs.
— Yiddish Proverb

Life is an adventure to be lived out every day that God gives us. Every day should include learning something new, working on acquiring a new skill, experiencing something new, some act that benefits someone and/ or prayer.

When I was a child, my life was like a puzzle, and how things fitted together was a mystery. Not until I finished acquiring enough knowledge in college and enough experience in the military, did the pieces of the puzzle fit together. Then I could understand how things worked and to know what I wanted to do - be a success at business, and what I wanted to accomplish - to be a faithful witness of Christ in the market place.

When Lura and I first met, she thought I was conceited, but it was the self-confidence I felt, a confidence that would provide her with the emotional stability that only a husband can provide. Joseph, of the Old Testament, was my role model for life. He was good with numbers, a planner, and a close advisor to Pharaoh and eventually earned the right to be in charge. My life followed his example.

MY PERSPECTIVES

What shaped me to be the person that I am? It was my God-given DNA and the people, experiences and training I had over a life-time. I am an optimist and planner by nature. My basic temperament is phlegmatic, but by training and experience I have become a more balanced personality. Using sheer will-power, I took Toastmasters and Dale Carnegie courses. Standing before a group of people was the last thing I wanted to do, but I learned how to do it and enjoy it. My leadership style is passive-aggressive, so I enjoy sitting back watching people, who have been under my coaching, succeed. There is nothing that gives me more satisfaction than seeing people realize their dreams. I am an aggressive thinker but conservative in my words and actions. That is why I don't make many major mistakes. I am sensitive enough not to put myself in an embarrassing spot.

In a given situation, I ask myself if time is working for me or against me. If it is working against me, I make a decision, and if it is working for me, I defer. I make a decision if it is routine or does not have significant implications, otherwise I defer. I enjoy games where there is an equal balance between strategy and chance. Strategy is the challenge and chance is the excitement. I avoid things that are pure chance, like the lottery.

After college I thought being rational was the only thing in life that mattered. Over the years I have discovered that there is an emotional content in everyone's life that drives them, and makes them tick. In my business I could work out clients financial and business problems without much difficulty, but it was all the other problems they had that gave me difficulty in advising them. The problems were of all kinds: divorce, drugs, death in the family, shopping addiction, anorexia/bulimia, partnership disagreements, evil spirits, rebellious children, atheism, and paranoia, just to name a few. In order to judge whether

I should advise a client or if a professional in that field should be engaged, I studied psychology and its application – counseling - at the Center for Biblical Counseling and the American Association of Christian Counselors, becoming a certified counselor.

One of the challenges of life is to avoid chasing skinny rabbits. A coyote chases a rabbit for miles, the rabbit darting back and forth, jumping over logs and cutting through underbrush, to evade him but is eventually caught. Then the coyote finds it is a skinny rabbit and he has burned up more energy in the chase than he gets eating the skinny rabbit. There are people who are dishonest, dysfunctional (going all through life and never able to get things to come out right), or just plain jerks (thinking they know everything but really are clueless). These people are skinny rabbits who will take 80% of your energy for 20% results.

I have described most of the influential people in my life but not all of them. Integrity is the essential foundation of relationships; friendships are built on mutual respect and love. I think of relationships as a series of rings: family, friends and acquaintances. Over the years we have spent enough time in various places to enlarge the friendship ring significantly, but my wife, children, grandchildren, son-in-law, daughter-in-law and deceased parents have meant the most to me.

Lura has been a faithful wife, partner, friend, supporter, counselor, encourager, housekeeper, and mother to our children, grandmother, and back-scratcher for over 50 years. A man could not ask for more. Her slight bent to being an obsessive-compulsive personality gives her the energy to set high standards and get things done right. Her rounded temperament makes her a warm and caring person and draws people to her. She is a godly woman, as good as the woman described in Proverbs, Chapter 31.

My life has been rich in experiences. Colleges, military service, corporate career, founding a business, church leadership, moving from city to city, vacations, foreign

My desire: To do life differently, raising the bar for personal growth

Therefore, if anyone is in Christ, he is a new creation; the old is gone, the new has come. II Cor. 5:17

What are the rewards of the challenge?

The peace of becoming more like Jesus.

And the peace of God, which transcends all understanding will Guard your hearts and your minds in Jesus Christ. Phil. 4:7

Joy of embracing a Christ-like lifestyle.

I have told you this so that my joy may be in you and that your joy may be complete. John 15:11

The confidence of being trained and equipped to live life well.

Being confident of this, that he who began a good work in you will carry it on to completion. Phil.1:6

The satisfaction of helping others through an overflowing gift-driven ministry.

Each one should use whatever gift he has received to serve others, faithfully administering God's grace in its various forms. 1 Peter 4:10

The excitement of helping seekers discover God.

Many of the Samaritans from that town believed in him because of the woman's testimony John 4:39

Love for people wherever they are on life's journey.

Accept one another, then, just as Christ accepted you, in order to bring praise to God. Romans 15:7 travel and family life have all added to enriching my life.

Life is all about learning and I have done it all my life. While I believe in working smarter rather than harder, most of my life has been spent working harder. The progression is knowledge — facts, understanding — how things work, and wisdom applying knowledge and understanding. I have studied at seven different colleges including Harvard School of Business, which was the best.

My desire: **Doing life differently by living it God's way**

I have fought the good fight, I have finished the race, I have kept the faith. Now there is in store for me the crown of righteousness. II Tim. 4: 7

To succeed and finish well, what kind of person should I want to be?

One who hungers for personal growth and has a healthy discontent with the status quo.

One who deeply desires God's best for his life.

One who wants to understand God's ways and then apply them in loving relationships and daily living.

One who is willing to under-go the challenge of personal life change.

One who has basic life skills for a well managed life with meaningful results, ministry and built-in margin to impact others.

One whose life in Christ overflows to have significant impact on others, so they can then come to know Him and grow in Him.

One who truly values relationships and intentionally builds them.

I have perused over 700 books, tapes and videos, which I have listed, and have built a library of books on many different subjects. Every year I have attended seminars or watched video classes. Yes, they are all recorded in my resume.

Life is about building a large mental database and then sorting it down in different ways for application. I have a large database, but it will all be gone three

---

My Desire: A challenging journey of unlimited opportunities

Blessed are those whose strength is in You, which have set their hearts on pilgrimage. Psalm 84:5

To take on the challenge, what kind of person should I want to be?

A person who daily cultivates a personal loving relationship with God, evidenced by His power and blessing.

For the Lord God is a sun and shield; the Lord bestows favor and honor; no good thing does he withhold from those whose walk is blameless. Psalms 84:11

A person who wants the values of relating to God to govern decision-making, possessions and relationships.

A person who has acquired a taste for positive change, the skills to manage it, and to understand the emotions that accompany it.

Continue to work out your own salvation with fear and trembling, for it is God who works in you to will and act according to his good purpose. Philippians 2:12 -13.

A person whose lifestyle is empowered by God's values, not driven by the culture.

minutes after I die, so I have tried to leave my story as a legacy.

The ability to plan is God given, just as God plans. Some claim that planning precludes God's control over our lives and actions, but planning is the application of wisdom. God does not control every moment of our lives but allows us the freedom to make decisions. God does promise to give us the wisdom, if we ask for it, to make decisions that honor his desires for us. Besides praying for wisdom, we can pray for God's intervention to change

---

The result: To be transformed by God's renewing of your mind.

A person who has mastered basic life skills to realize personal goals and whose priorities allow significant investment in helping others.

Do not conform any longer to the pattern of this world, but be Transformed by the renewing of your mind. Then you will be able to test and approve what God's will is—His good, pleasing and perfect will. Romans 12:2

A person who models God's love and grace and is willing to invest in relationship with people by cultivating, planting and reaping.

I have become all things to all men so that by all possible means. I might save some. I do all this for the sake of the gospel, that I may share in its blessings. I Corth. 9:22 -23

A person who values people as God sees them as precious, unique and of infinite value rather than as the world sees them in terms of race, gender and social status.

Filled with compassion, Jesus reached out his hand and touched the man. Mark 1 :41

the normal course of events or for a special sign of confirmation of his will. Even if we make bad decisions, He can make them come out for good, if we trust Him. As a planner my experience confirms this. My life is all about planning and wisdom.

Every year I write down what I want to accomplish during the next one to three years. I believe the only way to accomplish what is significant and meaningful, rather than letting life slip by one day at a time, is to measure. I have recorded our net worth and income every year for

To do that, what must I be?

A person who constantly seeks to know and understand the world they live in and its creator.

A person who cultivates an inquiring mind, learns from multiple sources and has an appetite for new experiences.

A person who is changing and, in turn, changing the world.

A person who loves to regularly worship, pray, integrate scripture and practice the presence of God.

A person who makes Biblically based life decisions, has a stewardship mentality and maintains integrity with others.

A person who is constantly integrating scriptural principles into godly relationships, applying skills and possessions to benefit others.

A person who has Biblically based good mental health and a positive view of the culture.

A person who has life goals with measurements, energy focused on realizing objectives and the peace of mind to let God and others deal with the rest of life.

A person who intentionally seeks out people who are not yet believers and builds relationships that are authentic for the purpose of introducing them to Christ fifty years. My plan was to have our net worth go up every day, every month and every year. Not all plans work perfectly, but our net worth has gone up almost every year because of saving and wise investing, so we still have every dollar of after-tax wages we have earned over a life-time. As Peter Drucker says, "What gets measured gets done." I have created a Family Time Line that records every significant event of our entire life and a Family Tree that records over fifteen hundred members of our extended family. This gives us a sense of family and of time.

Now this book records my life story. Planning and measurement are the keys to a good adventurous life, as long as it is God's plan.

MY CONCLUSIONS

I have been fortunate not to have made any major mistakes or had any significant trauma. God has given wisdom and led me in every significant decision and, for reasons only known to him, has spared me from pain or harm. There is nothing as uncertain as tomorrow, so we need to live for today and plan for tomorrow. Yesterday is gone forever, but it is the past that shapes us for the future. A Native American proverb says, "We will be known forever by the tracks we leave."

This is my life as I REMEMBER it.

LaVergne, TN USA
19 July 2010

190090LV00001B/2/P